TURNAROUND CHEFS

A recipe for change management

by

Ad van den Oord &
Arjan van den Born

ISBN: 9789082012323

Published by: Born To Grow (www.bornto.nl)

NUR-code: 801 (Management)

© 2014 J.A. van den Born / Ad van den Oord

ONTWERP: iborst@casema.nl

My Comfort Zone - A Poem

I used to have a comfort zone where I knew I wouldn't fail.
The same four walls and busywork were really more like jail.
I longed so much to do the things I'd never done before,
But stayed inside my comfort zone and paced the same old floor.

I said it didn't matter that I wasn't doing much.
I said I didn't care for things like commission checks and such.
I claimed to be so busy with the things inside the zone,
But deep inside I longed for something special of my own.

I couldn't let my life go by just watching others win.
I held my breath; I stepped outside and let the change begin.
I took a step and with new strength I'd never felt before,
I kissed my comfort zone goodbye and closed and locked the door.

If you're in a comfort zone, afraid to venture out,
Remember that all winners were at one time filled with doubt.
A step or two and words of praise can make your dreams come true.
Reach for your future with a smile; success is there for you!

Author Unknown

Contents

TURNAROUND CHEFS 1

PREFACE 7

INTRODUCTION 16

The Stages of Organizational Failure 20

The Process of Organizational TURNAROUND 27

I. ANATOMY OF A SUCCESSFUL RESTAURANT 35

X-factor 1: Passion, Hard Work & Discipline 45

X-factor 2: Care for Customers 50

X-factor 3: Stand out from the Crowd 54

X-factor 4: Ingenuity in Marketing 60

X-factor 5: Every Ship needs a Captain 64

X-factor 6: Focus on the Negatives 69

X-factor 7: Teamwork 73

X-factor 8: Keep It Simple Stupid 78

X-factor 9: Quality Control 82

X-factor 10: Business First 87

II. PRELIMINARIES TO CHANGE 91

Change Principle 1: All Change Comes From Within 92

Change Principle 2: All Change Triggers Resistance 100

III. DIAGNOSIS 105

Change Principle 3: Experience Being a Customer 111

Change Principle 4: Ask Your Customers 117

Change Principle 5: Observe Up Close and Personal 122

Change Principle 6: Put Pressure on the Organization 126

Change Principle 7: Bring In Outside Expertise 131

Change Principle 8: Get to the Bottom..135

Change Principle 9: Get Into the Mind of People 141

Change Principle 10: Understand the Business..146

IV. UNFREEZE..149

Change Principle 11: The Carrot … (create Hope for a Better Future) 154

Change Principle 12: And the Stick … (Confront with Undeniable Facts)..157

Change Principle 13: Internalize the Burning Platform 162

Change Principle 14: Be Provocative 168

Change Principle 15: Involve the Social Context..174

Change Principle 16: Test and Reward Fair Value 178

Change Principle 17: Communicate to the Soul 183

V. CHANGE..188

Change Principle 18: Ignite the Passion..192

Change Principle 19: Tough Love 197

Change Principle 20: Treat the Cause not the Symptom 203

Change Principle 21: Fast Follow-up 208

Change Principle 22: Teach your Children well 212

Change Principle 23: Laugh 217

Change Principle 24: Be Creative 221

Change Principle 25: Give the Right Person the Right Job 224

VI. FREEZE 229

Change Principle 26: Appoint Guards 232

Change Principle 27: Create Symbols of Successful Change 235

Change Principle 28: Validate the Change 238

Change Principle 29: Revisit Regularly 241

Change Principle 30: Give Fatherly Advice 243

VII. CONCLUSIONS 245

What can we learn from reality-TV? 248

A First on Organizational Pathology 265

Implications for Big Corporations 274

LITERATURE LIST 278

INDEX OF CITED RESTAURANTS 283

PREFACE

Many creative works are the expression of tension or frustration between what is expected and what is actually observed and this book is no exception. The idea for this book originated during an academic conference on organizational change in the city of Oranienburg, which is located about 20 kilometers from Berlin and infamous for the location of one of the first Nazi concentration camps. On a particular evening, while enjoying a local beer in a small pub, we (i.e., the authors) entered into a discussion about the gap between the academic theory and daily practice of organizational change. Of main interest was our observation that most academic studies on the subject do not (accurately) reflect many of the challenges encountered in change projects. Exploring the reasons for the mismatch between the theory and practice of organizational change an old parable came to mind, which is part of ancient Buddhist, Hindu, Sufi, and Jain teachings, and is called 'the blind men and the elephant'.

The Blind Men and the Elephant

Once upon a time, there lived six blind men in a village. One day the villagers told them, "Hey, there is an elephant in the village today." They had no idea what an elephant is, and decided, "Even though we would not be able to see it, let us go and feel it anyway." All of them went there, and touched the elephant. "Hey, the elephant is a pillar," said the first blind man who touched his leg. "Oh, no! It is like a rope," said the second blind man who touched the tail. "Oh, no! It is like a thick branch of a tree," said the third blind man who touched the trunk of the elephant. "It is like a big hand fan," said the fourth blind man who touched the ear of the elephant. "It is like a huge wall," said the fifth blind man who touched the belly of the elephant. "It is like a solid pipe," said the sixth blind man who touched the tusk of the elephant. They began to argue about the elephant and every one of them insisted that he was right, and they started to get agitated. A wise man was passing by and he saw this. He stopped and asked them, "What is the matter?" They said, "We cannot agree to what the elephant is like." Each one of them told what he thought the elephant was like. The wise man calmly explained to them, "All of you are right. The reason every one of you is telling it differently because each one of you touched the different part of the elephant. So, actually the elephant has all those features what you all said." "Oh!" everyone said. There was no more fight. They felt happy that they were all right (Jainworld, 2012).

Figure 1 The blind men and the elephant

This story is often used to provide insight into the relativity, opaqueness, or inexpressible nature of the truth, the behaviour of experts in fields where there is a deficit or inaccessibility of information, the need for communication, and respect for different perspectives (Wikipedia, 2012). In the context of our observation of a mismatch between theory and practice on organizational change, this parable can be interpreted as follows.

The academic approach is mainly analytical, which implies that the domain of investigation is divided into smaller elements or parts (e.g., natural science versus social science) to enable a detailed investigation (i.e., specialization) of the components parts to gain an understanding of the system as a whole (i.e., the elephant). Over time, further distinctions are made, and sub-disciplines emerge (e.g., social sciences is subdivided into economics, sociology, psychology, history, et cetera) that zoom in further and further on a particular subject or phenomena. Basically, an increasingly smaller part of science (i.e., the elephant) is studied, by creating more and more abstract concepts, categories, and theories. To increase progress, sub-disciplines are allowed to evolve autonomously (i.e., independent from one another), so that specific languages and methodologies can be developed for individual parts that enables scholars to specialize even further, to increase the efficiency of the investigation. However, over time, the language, methodologies, concepts, categories, and theories of individual disciplines drift further and further apart, until the basis of effective communication between disciplines is lost. Miscommunication arises that eventually results in conflict, and communication between disciplines effectively comes to a halt. Within science, unfortunately, there is no wise man that can effectively resolve the conflict between the disciplines. Hence, the current state of the social (organization) sciences can be characterized as one of fragmented development in isolated parts with little cross-fertilization between these parts (Daft and Lewin, 1990; van Witteloostuijn, 1995). In other words, there is much analysis (i.e., specialization) with little synthesis (i.e., generalization). The overall effect is that the practical relevance of academic research is somewhat lost. We think this is a pity as we are convinced that business could benefit from proper academic studies.

To prevent this partial view of reality, we decided to take a completely different approach to study organizational change. After all, we do not want to rely on the narrow confinements of a single discipline (or theory), but want to provide managers and entrepreneurs with a coherent view that transcends theoretical boundaries. We try

to accomplish this by applying the following threefold strategy, which is to (1) use grounded theory to distill the key principles by (2) using objective and controllable data, and (3) employing an analogy from medicine.

Grounded theory

Grounded theory is a scientific methodology in the social sciences involving the generation of theory from data (Glaser and Strauss, 1967). As such, it is a research method that operates almost in a reverse fashion from – what is now considered to be – traditional research. Traditional research starts by formulating a hypothesis (i.e., a theory fragment) and proceeds to collect data in an effort to prove the hypothesis (actually, the process is to disprove the opposite hypothesis; c.f., Popper, 2002). Instead, grounded theory starts with the collection of data through a variety of methods. This data is then coded and the codes are grouped into similar concepts in order to make them more workable. From these concepts, categories are formed, which form the basis for the creation of a theory, or a reverse engineered hypothesis. This contradicts the traditional model of research, where the researcher chooses a theoretical framework, and applies this model to the phenomenon to be studied (Wikipedia, 2012). However, like any theory or methodology, grounded theory is not without criticism. The main problem is that it is impossible to free oneself of preconceptions in the collection and analysis of data (Thomas and James, 2006). Although we fully agree with the fact that no one can ever be totally free from preconceived notions, we do think there are ways that this can be minimized. For example, by the collection of truly objective data and by using analogies from a different disciplines (like medicine in our case).

Truly objective and controllable data

Through the use of truly objective data, it is possible to minimize any preconceptions that might exist. Of course, even when the data itself is fully objective, there always remains a need to interpret the data, and our interpretations might also contain preconceived notions that bias our findings. Obviously, we cannot completely eliminate any distortion that is the result due to our subjective interpretation of the encountered data. However, what we can (and will) do is to use publicly available data that is extremely easy to access for any reader. This way, the reader has the possibility to access the data himself to validate or correct the interpretation that we have given to it. Thus, instead of trying to sell the reader a pre-cooked theory without access to the ingredients, we want to introduce our dish as well as the ingredients from which this dish was made. The reader can improve the dish by himself, by combining the ingredients in a (slightly) different way that better matches his or her reality (i.e., the reader can interpret the data in a different way). So, instead of the objective of trying to present a single, final theory, we want to provide food for thought, by providing the reader with the basic ingredients and a simple recipe how these ingredients can be combined to develop a nice dish or story.

The data that we will use in this book are episodes from reality TV-shows that have the objective to renew, transform, turnaround, or rescue (i.e., change) small businesses. Most of our observations, conclusions and examples are based on the show Kitchen Nightmares which stars top chef Gordon Ramsay. We have chosen this show for a number of reasons. First, Kitchen Nightmares and Gordon Ramsay kick-started this new genre of reality TV-shows on organizational turnaround. All reality TV-shows of this genre are based on the initial success of Kitchen Nightmares. Second, the show has been such a success that it is still running after eight years (since 2004). With almost 100 episodes (32 UK + 66 US), covering 83 restaurants in two countries it is arguably the show that is most powerful for academic analysis with plenty of testable data and information. Although we focused our research on Kitchen Nightmares (for which we have analyzed all episodes meticulously using video and timer), we sometimes refer to other reality TV-shows such as Restaurant Makeover and Tabatha Salon Takeover to compare Gordon Ramsay's behaviour and management style with these other TV-stars. Third, Kitchen Nightmares is a show dedicated to the restaurant business. We think this is an advantage as almost anybody can relate to the restaurant business, which makes it the ideal setting to explain our principles. Finally, we have chosen Kitchen Nightmares (UK and US) as our main subject of study because we believe, as the reader will see later, that Gordon Ramsay possesses skills that make him an extraordinary turnaround manager and a very interesting role model for practitioners of change management.

An important advantage of using entertaining TV-shows as our data source is that the reader can easily access the data to increase his or her understanding of the phenomenon that is explained. For this reason we want to give the following advice if you are really interested in organizational change: First, watch a number of episodes of Kitchen Nightmares (some UK and some US) before actually starting to read the book, as this will greatly enhance your insight and understanding of the concepts, notions, and theories we will explain in this book. In a manner of speaking, the book will come to life through the TV-show. Actually, the TV-shows and the book are complementary to one another. The book will increase the educational and entertainment value of the TV-show, and vice versa.

Medical analogy

The third way we try to transcend the theoretical boundaries of scientific theories on organizational change and minimize our preconceived notions is to use an analogy from medicine. More specifically, we will liken organizational failure to disease, and the process of organizational change to the treatment of the disease. By employing an analogy from a totally different discipline (i.e., medicine), we prevent a narrow interpretation of our findings due to the theoretical straightjacket that currently exists in organization science (Daft and Lewin, 1990) and is responsible for the huge gap that currently exists between theory and practice. That is, through the bricolage of concepts across disciplines and the usage of metaphors, new theories can be effectively conceived (Boxenbaum and Rouleau, 2011). In other words, by recombining concepts from different domains, we can generate theoretical innovations or novel recombinations (Schumpeter, 1934). Furthermore, the usage of analogies are a common problem solving strategy, as they provide a way of applying (mapping) known information (source) to novel problem solving domains (target), and are a great way to organize new and creative solutions.

Final words

Last, but not least, we want to communicate our deepest admiration for every entrepreneur. Creating a successful business isn't easy; it takes dedication, long hours and hard work to build a profitable enterprise. Life is also very hard for all those failing entrepreneurs. They wait for customers to show up, day after day, evening after evening. It takes strength and stamina to deal with this, and it is easy to lose enthusiasm and passion in these difficult and challenging situations. For that reason this book is primarily written for the entrepreneurs who are struggling, not only in the restaurant business, but in other industries as well.

Although we have written this book for entrepreneurs, we think this book is likewise advantageous to academics and experienced turnaround managers. Through our method of rigorous analysis and use of reality TV-shows the book adds many new ideas to the conventional wisdom on organizational change. Things that cannot be found in the academic literature nor in the practical management books on organizational turnarounds.

INTRODUCTION

Starting a new business is not an easy task; close to 50% of all new business fail within three years after coming into existence. The restaurant business, the industry on which we focus, is even more challenging, as almost 60% of all restaurants in the US close their doors within the same time span (Parsa et al, 2005). An important reason for this low survival rate is that many people start a restaurant (or business) for the wrong reasons (Schaeffer, 2011). This, as we will show, is clearly illustrated in the TV-show Kitchen Nightmares, which portrays many entrepreneurs who have fallen in love with the idea of owning a nice little restaurant, without realizing that running a restaurant requires a great deal of hard work and an astonishing level of commitment. For example, consider the story about Daniela, the owner of La Gondola.

La Gondola is an Italian restaurant in Derby, UK. Daniela, the current owner, fell in love with the restaurant during her teen years in the 1960s. At the time, La Gondola brought the glamour of Venice (Italy) to Derby. It had a wonderful atmosphere and an excellent reputation. According to Daniela, "In those days, the place was packed, and you had to book two to three weeks in advance to reserve a place." Daniela celebrated her 21st birthday and her marriage in the restaurant. In 2005, while going through some difficulties due to the death of her mother combined with a divorce, the dream of owning La Gondola was the only thing that kept her going, and before she realized it, she bought into her dream for half a million pounds. However, Daniela's delightful dream quickly turned into a horrible nightmare with empty seats and an incompetent and lazy staff, turning La Gondola into a financial fiasco.

As becomes painstakingly obvious by the above anecdote, having a dream of a successful restaurant is not quite the same as running one. Despite its laid back image, the restaurant business is extremely competitive with critical customers that judge performance solely on the basis of your last service, and customer loyalty is virtually non-existent. It is of the utmost importance to ensure that the quality of food and service can compete with nearby rivals. Moreover, besides hard work and a high level of commitment, one needs entrepreneurial and professional skills to keep the business afloat. Last but not least, the restaurants activities need to be organized and coordinated in such a way as to guarantee quality and avoid disappointment. After all, poor management is another major factor that contributes to business failure in the restaurant business (Parsa et al, 2005).

Running a restaurant is not rocket science, however, and more often than not a single visit to a failing restaurant reveals what is going wrong and how profitability can (easily) be improved. This raises an interesting question: If it is so blatantly obvious what is wrong with the restaurant, how is it possible that this flaw persists and why is it not properly dealt with by the owner or management? At first, we pondered that this could be caused by high workloads; owners (management) are too caught up in putting out small fires, which prevents him (them) from seeing the 'elephant' in the room. However, anyone that has been involved in a reorganization process or who has watched a couple of episodes of a TV-show on organizational turnarounds will tell you that, more often than not, the owner (or management) is told repeatedly and explicitly to change their erroneous ways by customers, staff, friends, and family. What then are the real causes that still prevents owners (management) from implementing the required changes to put the business back on track to prevent bankruptcy and financial disaster? As we will demonstrate later in this book, one of the main causes for this lack of initiative is that organizational change always implies individual change. Therefore, change generates uncertainty which results in great deals of anxiety, fear, frustration, and insecurity as the individual needs to step out of his/her comfort zone by changing old, worn-in, and ineffective – but comfortable – behavioural patterns. Not many individuals are ready for this task (i.e., to face their inner demons and insecurities), and often come up with the most creative excuses. It is for this reason that even in the prospect of impending doom or financial disaster owners (management) are reluctant to change. Hence, rigorous organizational change always carries a strong psychological component and individuals look for creative ways to sabotage the proposed changes to avoid being confronted with their own insecurities and inner demons.

Traditional models of organizational change do not pay much attention to the role of individual psychology, which is why they are often confronted by unexpected resistance and unforeseen attempts to sabotage the change process (e.g., by questioning the intent of the change or by attacking the change agent). In this book, we want to pay explicit attention to these phenomena, because insight into these phenomena enables us to anticipate and to effectively manage them. To do so, we will make the analogy between organizational failure and disease, which allows us to apply the doctrine from medicine to study organizational failure. More specifically, to emphasize the (individual) psychological component in organizational failure and change, we often draw on the analogy between organizational failure and mental disease. This also enables us to develop a fresh perspective to organizational failure and change, as we are not bound by traditional theories and preconceived notions on organizational failure and change.

THE STAGES OF ORGANIZATIONAL FAILURE

Before we can continue with the analogy between disease and organizational failure, we need to adapt the definition of disease to organizational failure. A disease is an abnormal condition affecting the body of an organism. Before we can apply this definition to organizations, we need to disambiguate the meaning of body. While creating the impression of something static, our body is actually a complex network of interdependent processes. Viewed in this manner, the definition can be easily adapted to organizations. Organizational failure (disease) is an abnormal condition affecting the complex network of interdependent processes (i.e., body) of an organization (i.e., organism). An abnormal condition implies that there is a deviation from the normal condition. Hence, there is an error in the functioning of the body, or complex web of interdependent processes. Treatment of the disease aims to alleviate this error through surgery or medicine. In the case of organizational failure, the aim is to alleviate this error through the implementation of organizational change.

Organizational change is a rather vague concept. A literal interpretation can basically refer to any change in an organization. This can range from the sale of a single product to the evolution from a sole proprietorship into a large multinational enterprise (MNE). We thus need to define the concept of organizational change before we continue. We define organizational change as the intentional change of the organization to increase its performance. Performance is a multidimensional concept, and its precise definition and the way in which it is measured depends upon the actual viewpoint taken. To define our performance measure, we actually approach the issue from the opposite direction, which is also in line with our medical analogy. The most dramatic outcome of any disease is when the individual person dies from his disease. The most dramatic outcome for a failing organization is organizational death, which means that the organization is disbanded and ceases to exist. This means that the ultimate performance measure (i.e., the one that counts the most) of any organization is organizational survival. Organizational change can now be defined as the intentional change of the organization to increase the organization's likelihood of survival (by decreasing its hazard or risk of mortality).

Prosperity

Birth ● ⟵⟶ Mediocrity

Failure

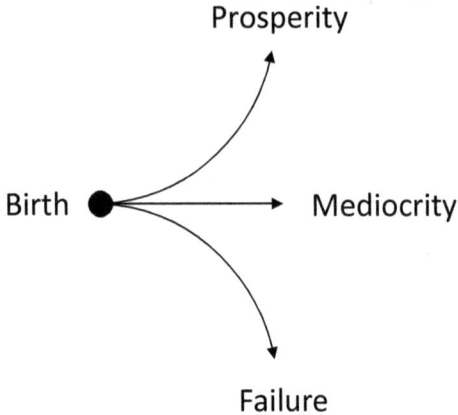

Figure 2 Organizational evolution

When considering the evolution (or change) of an organization, three basic scenarios emerge: (1) prosperity, (2) mediocrity, and (3) failure or decline (see Figure 2). Prosperity implies that the positive forces in the organization are stronger than the negative forces, and are driving the organization forward towards the goals that it has set for itself (see Figure 3). That is, the organization evolves with its customers through small incremental changes implemented by its employees and management to increase the profitability of the organization. This is called continuous corporate renewal, and is the most relaxed form of organizational change, with no need for outside help.

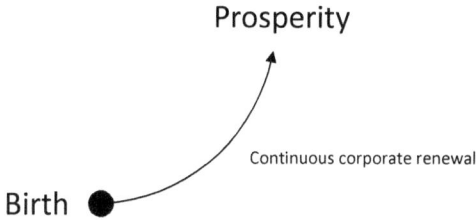

Figure 3 The road to organizational prosperity

Mediocrity refers to the situation where the organization does not prosper and does not fail, which means that organizational performance is stable. While it does not get any better, it also does not get any worse. The positive and negative forces within the organization are in balance. To travel the path of prosperity, continuous corporate renewal needs to be (re)-installed, and this can be accomplished either with or without outside help.

If an organization is failing, the negative forces are pulling the organization down, and positive forces are largely absent. According to Weitzel and Johnson (1989), different stages or phases can be identified on the road to organizational demise, which are defined as follows: (1) *blinded* – failure to anticipate or detect negative forces, (2) *inaction* – failure to take on corrective action despite signs of deteriorating performance, (3) *faulty action* – faulty decisions and/or faulty implementation of decisions while failure becomes overt, (4) *crisis* – failed efforts result in chaos and panic within the organization, (5) *dissolution* – irreversible stage leading to organizational death. See Figure 4.

Birth ●————— 1. Blinded

2. Inaction

3. Faulty action

4. Crisis

5. Dissolution

Failure

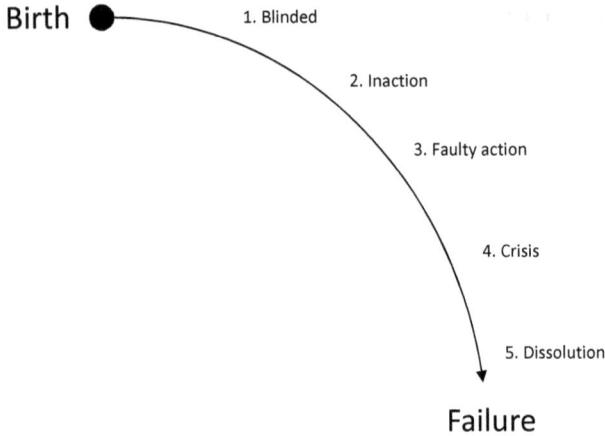

Figure 4 The road to organizational failure

Organizational adaptation (can be compared to applying an ointment)
Obviously, the type of organization change that is needed to restore health depends upon the stage of failure or decline. In the blinded stage, what is needed is to re-(install) organizational awareness or sensitivity so that the early warning signs of the negative forces are observed and action can be taken to combat them. This basically implies making moderate changes in the internal and external monitoring systems (Weitzel and Johnson, 1989). Failure to take action in this stage means that the organization will slide into the stage of inaction.

Organizational transformation (can be compared to stitching)
In the stage of inaction, the negative effects become noticeable, as the performance of the organization begins to decline. While the company is likely to remain fundamentally

sound, problems have grown to the point where they cannot be denied (Shein, 2011). However, despite these signs, organizational leaders delay corrective action because, on the one hand, change is costly and, on the other hand, they might believe the threat is merely of a temporary nature. To restore health, a transformation is needed that requires making larger change in the organization, to combat underperformance in a certain domain, aspect, or level of the organization. At this stage, although the organization's financial picture is probably worsening, there is still no pressing financial need to improve the business. Change is still of an incremental nature and the need for outside help is medium.

Turnaround management (can be compared to surgery)
By now, the failure becomes highly overt and noticeable, and the financial situation is deteriorating due the organization's severe underperformance. Organizational leaders finally become active, and decide to combat the worsening situation. Faulty decisions and/or faulty implementation lead to faulty action, threatening the organization's viability even further. By now, failure has spread throughout the organization and radical changes are needed to restore the organization's health. To turn the organization around, rapid action is needed in multiple domains and at multiple levels, and the need for outside help become high.

Organizational rescue (can be compared to intensive care)
Failure to turn the organization around implies that the organization will slide into a stage of crisis, as chaos and panic wreak havoc throughout the organization. At this junction, there is one final chance left to bring the organization back to life, and prevent it from going belly-up. Chances of survival are pretty slim, as the organization

can no longer meet its financial obligations, such as the payment of salary, debt, and taxes. The organization's survival is basically dependent upon the willingness of the organization's stakeholders (e.g., fiscal department, employees, suppliers, et cetera) to restructure its debt. This is the most drastic form of organizational change, as it requires immediate action to prevent the organization from bankruptcy. As the whole organization needs to be restructured, change is of a highly radical nature and outside help has become a necessity.

While the skills and capabilities of a change agent are to a large extent dependent upon the kind of organizational changes that are needed, many of the principles are universal in every type of change; from adaptation to rescue. The main difference between these types of changes lies in the extent of the required changes and in the time that is available to make these changes (and this sense of urgency results from short time frames). In dire straits, a turnaround or rescue manager needs to make lot of radical changes in a very short period of time to save the business from impending doom. There is little room for negotiation and the core of the organization needs to be changed; i.e., the identity of the organization and the people need to be reinvented in such a way that the organization establishes a positive cash flow to pay off the existing debt. This is not easy and, as we will see, it will take an extensive toolbox and extraordinary personality to accomplish this difficult task. In the remainder of this book, we mainly focus on the process of organization turnaround for two obvious reasons. First, most restaurants in Kitchen Nightmares are in this stage of development. Second, organizational turnaround's main focus is on the internal working of the organization, while organizational rescue also has a strong focus on the external environment of the organization, in the restructuring of debt.

THE PROCESS OF ORGANIZATIONAL TURNAROUND

The framework of this book is based on two grand theories of change, one from the world of psychology, the other one comes originally from the world of engineering. From psychology we take the long-standing and famous theory of Kurt Lewin (1947) as a starting point. Lewin explains change as a three stage process (Figure 5). The first stage of change ("Unfreeze") involves overcoming inertia and dismantling the existing mind set. It is in this stage that defense mechanisms have to be bypassed. In the second stage ("Change") the actual adjustments are implemented. In the third and final stage ("Freeze") the new mindset is crystallized and one's comfort level is returned to previous levels. From engineering we used classical control theory (i.e., cybernetics). This field of study deals with the behaviour of dynamic systems (Åström & Murray, 2008). The objective of control theory is to plan and execute corrective action to ensure system stability. A car's cruise control is a great example of such a control system. In a cruise control system, a sensor monitors the car's speed and feeds this information to a controller which adjusts the throttle as necessary to match the car's speed with the ideal speed. Now when the car goes uphill a decrease in speed is measured, and the throttle position changed to increase engine power, speeding the vehicle. Feedback from measuring the car's speed has allowed the controller to dynamically compensate for changes to the car's speed.

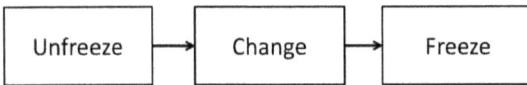

Figure 5 Kurt Lewin's three-stage change process (1947)

What happens in cruise control is quite comparable to what takes place in organizational turnaround. Similar to a cruise control system, a turnaround manager defines an ideal state (for a business), measures the actual situation (of the business), and compares the actual situation with the ideal or desired state/behaviour (Figure 6). Then, the turnaround manager decides on the necessary correcting actions to get closer to the ideal state. In system language, the turnaround manager acts as the feedback controller. He or she keeps correcting the situation until it is close enough to the ideal situation or further change is simply not realizable. The turnaround manager will then exit the process (i.e., the turnaround).

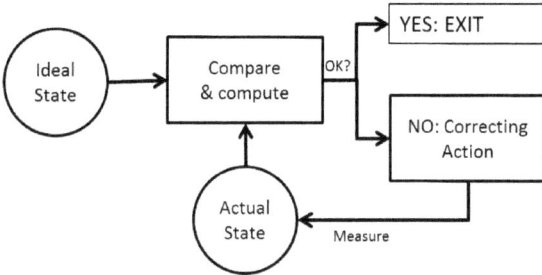

Figure 6 Feedback loop in control systems (Wikipedia)

In Figure 7, we combine the dynamics of system theory (Figure 6) with Lewin's model of change (Figure 5) thus creating a dynamic feedback model of organizational change. There are three differences between classical control theory and our dynamic model of organizational change. First, exiting an organizational turnaround cannot be done without freezing (i.e., institutionalizing the change). Second, change is a two-step process. The first step is to unfreeze the object (organization or individual), and the second step is to actually changing the object. In general, the turnaround manager cannot immediately change the situation. Three, our model is considerably more complex than standard control systems which have a single-input and single-output (SISO) such as a cruise control with single-input (speed) and single-output (throttle). Many different aspects of an organization have to be constantly measured (e.g., leadership, structure, control, procedures, behaviour, et cetera) and controlled. In control theory such a dynamic model with multi-inputs and multi-outputs is called a MIMO model (Wikipedia, 2012).

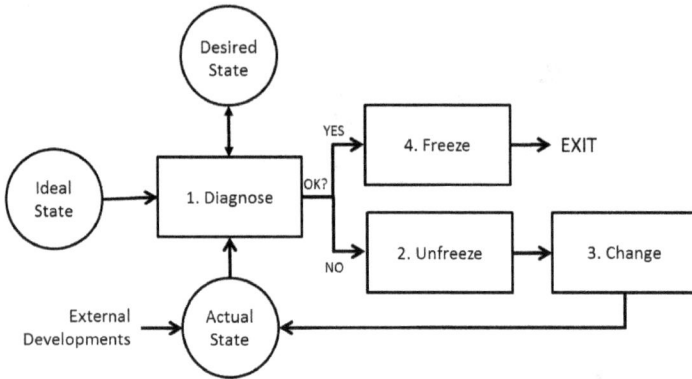

Figure 7 A dynamic control model of turnaround management

These three adjustments lead to a rudimentary model of organizational change that despite its simplicity is very capable of creating complex and seemingly chaotic patterns. There are three features in our model which collectively determine whether (i) the business will reach a higher level of sustained profitability or (ii) uncontrolled chaos and failure will emerge. These features are very much related to the skills of the turnaround manager. Firstly, it is important that the change or leap forward is 'doable'. This means that the turnaround manager should be able to define a desired state (of increased profitability) that is reachable for the organization and its individuals given the actual state of affairs. This desired state does not equal the ideal state, as the ideal state is often not realistic given the actual state of the business. The desired state is thus constructed by applying common sense to the comparison of actual state with the ideal state. For example, a mediocre chef will never be able to run the kitchen of a distinguished Michelin-star restaurant. This is obviously not a realistic end-state. But such a chef is probably quite able to manage the kitchen of a great cafeteria or bistro. If the turnaround manager defines a desired state that cannot be attained (e.g., given the actual state and the change capacity of the organization and its individuals), the model will never find an equilibrium on a higher plateau, but oscillates between different kinds of changes. In this case, the turnaround effort will only lead to chaos and failure. Secondly, the turnaround manager has to constantly measure a whole set of different indicators to determine whether the restaurant is moving closer to this desired state or not and whether corrective action is needed. If the turnaround manager is not measuring frequently and sufficiently, the chances are that the whole system will fall apart leading again to chaotic organizational failure. In practice this means that a turnaround manager has to be present. His presence is needed, especially in areas where problems may arise. Thirdly, the turnaround manager must be able to figure out which type of corrective action is needed (i.e., unfreezing, changing, or freezing) to bring the whole system closer to a new equilibrium on a higher level. If the turnaround manager is not able to select and implement the right actions, the model will not return to equilibrium. Again the model will spin out of control as erroneous actions of the turnaround manager will lead to resistance and create an actual state that is even worse than the initial state. The organization will be like a car with a broken down cruise control; stopping in the middle of the high-way and speeding up in the car park. The lack of skills of the turnaround manager is the fundamental reason why so many turnarounds are considered to be chaotic processes.

The contents of this book

This book identifies and defines the utensils in the change toolbox in seven chapters. These seven chapters each represent a building block of our dynamic control model of turnaround management. In the first chapter, *The Autonomy of a Successful Restaurant*, we will discuss the fundamental elements of a successful restaurant business. Jointly, these elements form the yardstick to which a turnaround manager compares each restaurant from the moment he or she enters it; the so-called ideal state. The first chapter is therefore very different from the other chapters. While the subsequent chapters focus on the turnaround process of change and resistance, the first chapter merely describes the perfect restaurant. In this imaginary restaurant, the owners and cooks are passionate about food, care about their customers, and closely work together as a team understanding each other's strength and weaknesses. Such a restaurant continually develops its level of expertise and goes from strength to strength. Alas, these perfect restaurants do not appear in our TV shows. In these TV shows only faulty restaurants with many weaknesses can be seen. Thus the ultimate restaurant described in the first chapter is largely based on the improvements the turnaround manager realizes in the various restaurants, and the comments he makes about the flaws of the restaurants we do encounter. However this chapter is important because it helps the reader to understand the changes the turnaround manager needs to make in order to create a profitable business.

In the second chapter, *Preliminaries to Change*, we leave our description of the ideal restaurant and enter a world where owners are in denial, chefs have a distorted view of reality, people work against each other, cooperation is in short supply, and misinterpretation and disorganization are abundant. Before entering this snake pit, it is important that we discuss the 'contract' between the restaurateur and turnaround manager, to avoid being bitten by poisoned snakes before work actually begins. Some of the questions that are important in this respect are: What kind of help do they need? What does the turnaround manager need in return?

The third chapter, *Diagnosis*, is basically about the techniques a turnaround manager uses to really understand the cause(s) of the main problems of the restaurant that need to be treated or changed. In other words, what are the biggest problems of the restaurant, what causes these problems, how can the turnaround manager discover them, and how can he develop a thorough understanding about them in a rather short time span?

In a failing restaurant, owners and management have often developed a strong defense mechanism to resist change. To enable change in such a setting, you first have to bring these defenses down. Often, this can only be accomplished by explicit confrontation in a 'battle of wills', to shatter them completely. Of course, ripping existing ways of thinking to pieces is not the ultimate goal of a turnaround manager, but merely an intermediate stage of the turnaround process before real changes can be implemented in the restaurant. In the fourth chapter, *Unfreeze*, we discuss the techniques that are used to dismantle existing ways of thinking (Lewin, 1947).

The fifth chapter, *Change*, shows how the turnaround manager can turn the business, its owners, and other members of staff around. We also discuss resistance to change, because resistance often results in failure of many change initiatives. Resistance affects all stages of the turnaround process, which means that it is not sufficient to merely bring down defenses in the initial *unfreeze* stage of the turnaround process. Instead, the turnaround manager should be wary during all stages, as even the infinitesimal change (e.g., the addition of a new dish to the menu or the removal of a painting on the wall) can trigger resistance and lead to colossal confrontations with owners and chefs. Resistance to change is not always a bad thing (Ford & Ford, 2009), though, as it also prevents decay and provides consistency of behaviour. Resistance is most dangerous when it is based on personal motives and not in the best interest of the restaurant. In chapter five, we discuss the various sorts of resistance, and how to best deal with them.

Chapter six, *Freeze*, describes the final step of the turnaround process, where the turnaround manager tries to consolidate the change. In this refreezing phase, the turnaround manager tries to prevent a return of the restaurant to its old ways through a wide array of quite simple techniques. Although the techniques of chapter six are not as complicated as those described in the earlier chapters, they are very important. Even so many change managers tend to disregard this vital step. They have done their work, but without paying some minimal attention to securing the results and ensuring that the change effort does not regress to the old state.

Finally chapter seven talks about our conclusions. After watching over 100 TV-shows we deduced the typical pathology of organizational change. In this chapter we discuss how its conclusions differ from academic work and practitioners handbooks on organizational change. We feel that our approach based on grounded theory and using the medical analogy as well as objective data (i.e., TV-shows) adds a lot of value and brings significant new insights. Finally chapter seven also discusses the role, ideal profile and the necessary competences of a turnaround manager. This is not only based on the successes of these TV-stars, but also on their failures as some restaurants, such as The Walnut Tree, Piccolo Teatro, Seascape, Sebastian's, and Lela's, were not turned around. This observation points to the fact that a turnaround manager cannot always win. Just as a doctor and psychologist, you cannot cure all your patients.

I. ANATOMY OF A SUCCESSFUL RESTAURANT

When diagnosing and/or treating a patient, the doctor needs to be aware of the anatomy of a healthy individual. This is, however, not an easy task, as no two individuals are ever completely alike. So, how is the doctor able to distinguish between normal variation between individuals and abnormal variation due to disease and illness? In essence, this is a matter of experience. Over the years, the states of healthy and sick individuals has been documented and recorded, and diseases have been identified, described, and classified. This has led to the development of indicators and rules of thumb to identify diseases and distinguish between normal and abnormal states of the human body. Furthermore, remedies and medicines have been invented, discovered, and developed to treat the disease or illness (i.e., to bring the abnormal state of the human body back to normality). Hence, doctors are trained and educated for many years to become acquainted with the normal and abnormal states of the human body, by studying – amongst others – human anatomy, physiology, and pathology. Furthermore, they also have to put the theory into practice during several years of applied practice. In other words, doctors in training are first taught the theory of medicine and then have to apply this theory in practice to build the competence and experience needed to effectively treat patients and cure diseases. Doctors thus rely on the accumulated knowledge and experience of practitioners that have gone before him from books, coaching, and training.

The history of medicine

The history of medicine goes back many years. The ancient Egyptians already had a system of medicine that was well ahead of its time and which has strongly influenced later medical traditions, and the earliest know surgery was performed in Egypt around 2750 BC. The high priest Imhotep, who was the chancellor of Pharao Djoser during the 3rd dynasty of Egypt, is regarded by some as the founder of ancient Egyptian medicine and the original author of the Edwin Smith Papyrus, which is an ancient textbook on surgery that describes in detail the examination, diagnosis, treatment, and prognosis of numerous ailments (Britannica, 2012a). Another important figure in the history of medicine is the physician Hippocrates of Kos (460 BC to 375 BC), who is considered the "father of modern medicine" (Britannica, 2012b). The Hippocratic Corpus is a collection of around seventy early medical works from ancient Greece strongly associated with Hippocrates and his students. Most famously, Hippocrates invented the Hippocratic Oath for physicians, which is still relevant and in use today.

The history of organization

The history of organization also dates back a long time. For example, the division of labor (i.e., job specialization), along with tools, a more complex brain structure, and linguistic communication has been responsible for starting the human conquest of nature, and started over thousands of years ago. The history of the modern organizations originated a little bit over 600 years, when the Venetians (around 1400 AD) developed a primitive version of the car assembly line, as they floated warships down waterways, stopping them at different location to add another essential part or piece of equipment to the ships. Things really took off during the industrial revolution, which was only possible through the division of labor. This concept of labor division was given theoretical birth in 1776, when the father of modern economics and capitalism, Adam Smith, detailed the drastic productivity increase that can be accomplished through the breakdown of jobs into narrow and repetitive tasks that allows individuals to become skilled in their task (Smith, 1977).

While the history of organization has been well documented, the concept of organizational development and change is only a recent phenomenon. Organizational development is defined as "an effort, planned, organization-wide, and managed from the top, to increase organization effectiveness and health through planned interventions in the organization's processes, using behavioural-science knowledge" (Beckhard, 1969). Throughout the 1970s and 1980s organizational development became a more established field with courses and programs being offered in business, education, and administration curricula. In the 1990s and 2000s, organizational development continued to grow and evolve and its influences can be seen in theories and strategies such as total quality management (TQM), team building, job enrichment, and business process reengineering (BPR). By now, organizational development is known as both a field of applied behavioural science focused on understanding and managing organizational change and as a field of scientific study and inquiry. It is interdisciplinary in nature and draws on sociology, psychology, and theories of motivation, learning, and personality (Helms ed., 2006).

Due to its rather short history, practitioners of organizational turnaround and rescue do not have a large body of knowledge and experience to rely upon. What further complicates matters is the state of science (cf. the parable of the blind men and the elephant in the preface). Due to the focus on specialization in science, the disciplines that make up organizational development are not integrated. The result is that the domain of organizational development and change is rather fragmented and composed of many so-called experts that merely apply one or two principles from one of the scientific domains it builds upon, without much emphasis on the whole. In other words, a holistic perspective is largely absent.

This state of affairs can be compared with the state of affairs before medicine became a formal discipline. Before being a formal and licensed discipline, not all so-called experts were practicing medicine in an effort to heal people, as many of them merely 'practiced' medicine to generate income and fame. The strategy of these charlatans was to provide quick fixes or the mere impression of a quick fix by working on the psychology of the patient to increase personal wealth. The reason why they could employ such strategies is because it is relatively easy to combat symptoms and hereby give the impression of a cure, without actually combating the true cause of the disease. After all, the placebo effect is well documented in scientific research, and, according to a recent article in

Scientific American, placebos have helped to alleviate pain, depression, anxiety, Parkinson's disease, inflammatory disorders, and even cancer (Niemi, 2009). In a study of patients suffering from irritable bowel syndrome, the placebo effect even provides an 'adequate relief of symptoms' to 62% of all patients (Katchup et al., 2008). The placebo effect basically refers to the power of our beliefs in curing ailments. However, what happens when the treatment with the placebo stops, the disease lingers on, and patients revert to their old beliefs? For this reason, charlatans of the old age generally did not linger at the scene, and instead made sure that they are far one before the symptoms come back, and the patient eventually dies. Now, let us consider so-called organizational change experts or consultants again. Usually, they also visit the organization for a rather short period of time. So, they too are long gone before symptoms reappear and the organization is heading for disaster. And, as organizational development and change it is still more of an art than a science, it is always possible to attribute eventual failure to wrong implementation of the proposed solutions.

After this warning on the charlatans of organizational development and change, let us consider some positive aspects that we can learn by comparing the evolution of organizational development and change to the history of medicine. In our opinion, what is needed in organizational change and development is a clear image of a healthy organization, which enables identifying unhealthy organizations. This means that we first need to identify normal behaviour, so that abnormal deviations can be easily detected. Hence, in this chapter, we develop the anatomy of a successful restaurant. On the basis of this image, we can then identify restaurant disease and failure. Over time, different types of diseases and failure can be identified, and remedies and medicines can be developed.

Anatomy of a restaurant

Let us start by investigating successful restaurants. First of all, we can identity different kinds of successful restaurants. For example you may own a successful three-star Michelin restaurant, a thriving bistro, a profitable fine dining restaurant, a lucrative hamburger joint, or a prosperous pub. Different types of restaurants have somewhat different business models. Restaurants that offer fine dining should excel in food, have a great wine-list, and provide a relaxing ambiance in order to build a strong reputation and persuade customers to spend money. For a fish and chips eatery these capabilities are not crucial. Here it is much more important to turn tables fast in order to get as many people in as possible. In such a restaurant the combination of low price and limited margins coupled by high utilization rates lead to profitability. Nevertheless, there are some essential aspects or basic ingredients that should be found in any successful restaurant. This chapter discusses ten basic ingredients of flourishing restaurants. These ten ingredients have to work together in order for a restaurant to be profitable. But, as with any dish, some ingredients are more important than others. If a vital ingredient is missing, the restaurant could go bankrupt. If a minor ingredient is missing, the restaurant will simply not live up to its full potential.

Before we discuss the ten basic ingredients, we have to inform the reader about the typical configuration of a restaurant. The restaurant business is essentially a people business. A restaurant owner cannot do it all alone. There needs to be a team, each person bringing in personal knowledge and experience. To understand turnarounds in the restaurant business, we need to shed some light on the most important people in a restaurant. In Figure 8, the basic lay-out of a restaurant is depicted. It shows that a restaurant is basically a three man band, which means that there are three key people that determine the success of the restaurant. First, and foremost, is the owner and leader of the restaurant. This is the person who runs entrepreneurial risks, and the person who gets the profits when the restaurant is successful. This person also has the ultimate responsibility for running the restaurant, changing the restaurant as well as hiring and firing people. Behind the owner, the second most important person in the restaurant is the chef. He is responsible for creating the menu and running the kitchen. He buys the ingredients, cleans the kitchen, and is responsible for all things concerning food. He is also responsible for the kitchen staff and teamwork, cooperation, and communication in the kitchen. The final person in this business triangle is the maître d'hôtel or head waiter, or in short, the maître-d. This person is responsible for running the members of staff serving the customers. It is a very simple structure with very clear roles and responsibilities.

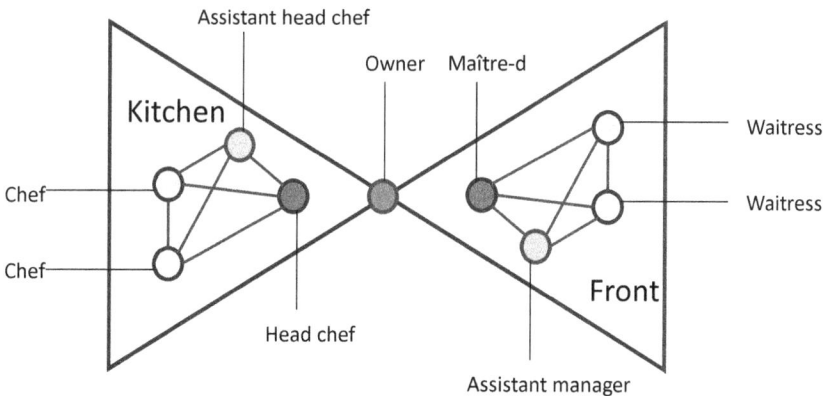

Figure 8 The basic lay-out of a restaurant

It is not uncommon in the restaurant business that the owner has multiple roles. The person can act as chef and owner, or as owner and maître-d. In these cases the three man band is reduced to a duo. This alternative configuration does not change the conclusions of this book. It is merely the case that it is sometimes demanding for a person to play two totally different roles. What is important, as we will see in the chapters on change, is that the top team is aligned.

With a specific role come certain requirements. Let's start with what is expected of an owner. With ownership comes the responsibility for your restaurant and your staff. You should be able to look objectively at your restaurant and your staff, and you should not hesitate to make the right decisions. Unfortunately, many of the failing restaurants are led by people who do not want or dare to lead. They typically want to be friends with their staff and they are afraid to bring necessary, but unpleasant messages. This is not good. As an owner you need to understand that you need to stand apart from your staff and that it is tricky to be intimate friends with your staff. It is sometimes lonely at the top.

The chef, more than anything else, should be a master in the kitchen. This seems obvious, but as Gordon Ramsay notes in the episode on restaurant The Dovecote Bistro in Devon, England: "I am always amazed how many small restaurants have the wrong people in the kitchen." This is not to say that every cook should be able to cook at Michelin star level, but rudimentary cooking skills are essential. But being a chef is about so much more than simply being a good cook. A great chef should also be able to run the kitchen in its broadest sense. This implies motivating and challenging the kitchen staff (i.e., sous-chef and junior staff members), and cooperating with the maître-d who runs the front of house staff. The role of the chef is perhaps even more important during service. Communication skills are essential during this period, as the slightest miscommunication can lead to gigantic blunders.

The role of front-of-house staff is not easy. They have to work the tables (sell specials, sell the wine), be friendly, show affection, and manage the flow of orders into the kitchen. The front-of-house is often an underestimated task. The maître-d or host is responsible for running the front-of-house staff, maintain service levels, creating a welcoming and friendly atmosphere, and flawless communication to the kitchen. A great maître-d is a "people person" with great customer service skills. The perfect maître-d is highly organized, has great leadership and communication skills, is a good listener, and must be able to negotiate and problem-solve. Last but not least, the maître-d must also possess numerical skills in the event he or she must operate the cash register.

The basic restaurant structure and roles are thus very simple. But it is here that many of the crucial mistakes are made. As we will see, many restaurants have unclear roles and responsibilities, and nobody knows exactly who is responsible for what. In other restaurants we observe people that are unfit for their roles; owners who do not lead, chefs who cannot cook, and obnoxious maître-d's. To be a top performing team, the organization and communication should be perfect. People should possess the right skills, understand not only who is responsible for what, but also how work is coordinated, and what to do when things go askew.

Next, we will discuss the basic ingredients of a successful restaurant in the following chapter, *Anatomy of a Successful Restaurant*. Every paragraph describes a certain quality or X-factor in detail and we show how it affects business performance. Every paragraph has the same outline; we start with a scene from Kitchen Nightmares to illustrate the practical importance of a particular X-factor. Subsequently we explain the academic theory behind the X-factor and give some additional examples from Kitchen Nightmares to clarify our argument further. We end every section with an example of this X-factor from outside the restaurant business. This final illustration is given to explain the generic importance of this quality for all businesses.

X-factor 1: Passion, Hard Work & Discipline

Have you lost the passion? Gordon asks Brian, the chef from Momma Cherri's Soul Food Shack. Brian has the makings of a talented cook, but his skill has not been tested for a long time, because the owner of the restaurant, Charita, wants to do the cooking herself. Brian's only job is to get precooked meals out of one of the 13 freezers in the kitchen and then heat them in the microwave. Charita has hired him as a chef, but she does the cooking of the food herself and composes the menu. In such a work environment it is no surprise that Brian is regularly late for work. There is no reason for being early if the work is that undemanding. Gradually, Brian has taken up another role; the role of the parent. At home he takes care of his children in the morning so his wife can go to work early. He sees his job as something that brings in money, but not as something that motivates him. Cooking does not play a central role in his life. He has lost his passion for food and his motivation for cooking.

Daniel Pink (2011) shows that true passion is related to autonomy, mastery, and purpose. People are passionate about their profession: (1) if they can make their own choices in the workplace – and be accountable for them, (2) if they are able to get better at something that matters to them, and (3) if they do this in the service of something larger than themselves. Preventing chefs to become better in their trade, cooking, will not only eradicate their passion, but will also diminish the chances of success of the restaurant. If you are not challenged by your work each and every day, you will lose your motivation sooner or later. When people are not challenged by their tasks, this will inevitably leads to apathy and boredom (Csíkszentmihályi, 1997).

There are many restaurant owners who are not in it for the passion of the business, but for other reasons, such as, money, ego, and the romantic idea of running a restaurant. A good example of a person who is in love with his own ego is Alex, the owner and chef of restaurant La Lanterna. He is very proud of himself, he wears a fancy cook uniform with "Chef Executive" embroidered on it and drives a brand new BMW with personalized plates "A1 6HEF." He has invested more money in his personal image than in cooking. He himself is his passion. Cooking is definitely not. Another good example of a big ego is Peter from Peter's restaurant in Babylon, New York. Peter explains: "I take care of myself and it shows, instead of a stove I bought a suit."

It is fascinating that so many starting restaurant owners think that running a restaurant is like being on holiday. Take the example of Peter and Louise Hamilton-Slade. They have used their life savings to buy The Sandgate Hotel. When they bought the hotel they instructed the staff that the hotel should be operated as if it was a holiday cottage. The owners wanted to eat, drink, and be happy. "My brief when I started here is to run it like it was their lounge," Stuart, the manager of The Sangate Hotel, told Gordon Ramsay. Needless to say that the hotel came spiraling down on them. Running a restaurant is not a laidback lifestyle, it's a serious job. It is a business venture, not a romantic get-together with friends and family. If you want to see your friends, throw a party. Don't invest your live savings into a business if you have no intention of managing it.

Running a restaurant is perhaps one of the toughest jobs out there. It is no fun, but hard work and a lot of stress. Owning a restaurant means you will be at work the majority of the time, especially in the beginning. You need to work weekends, holidays, and on your kids' birthdays. A restaurant owner can earn a decent living only if he or she is willing to work hard; cooking, managing and waiting tables. You need to be able to answer the phone, take care of (disgruntled) customers, fix broken equipment, track inventory, and pay rent as well as other suppliers. Typically restaurants can't support dead weight for very long. Moreover, if the business slows down, the owner is the first to go without a pay-check. Then there is the constant stress; when its busy you worry about the staff's service, when it's slow you worry about money.

One needs to understand the harshness of the restaurant business to appreciate the importance of passion. Without passion, it is impossible to put in the required effort. Unfortunately passion for food is by no means enough. Of course, doing something that you truly love can encourage you to work hard. But remember that cooking for friends and family is not the same as cooking for strangers who are paying money for your food. Often the best way to ruin your preferred pastime is to make it your living. You must therefore combine passion with discipline. This is especially important if you do not fully master the restaurant business when you start. You will only create a successful restaurant through an enormous amount of hard, demanding, and painful work over many years.

Previous entrepreneurial success in another business is also no guarantee for success in the restaurant business. In our reality TV shows there are many business owners that are (or have been) successful in another trade. A case in point is successful entrepreneur Nigel Nieddu, who opened The Granary, an upscale restaurant with 200 seats in rural Hampshire (he actually takes Gordon Ramsay on a tour of the grounds of his restaurant in his own private helicopter). The owner is hugely successful in other ventures, but cannot figure out why his restaurant is doing so poorly. As so often, the biggest problem is uncalled-for pride. Nigel thinks that, because he was successful in other areas, he is also naturally successful in the restaurant business, despite having zero experience in it. Consequently, any suggestions to change are taken as personal affront, rather than valuable advice.

The importance of passion is not only crucial in the restaurant business. The future belongs to the passionate in all industries. Only companies which are passionate about what they do and why they do it are able to put enough time and energy to constantly improve products and service. Look at the company that has perhaps set today's standard of passion: Apple. Apple has been able to redefine music distribution with its iPod and iTunes, created a new class of mobile phones with the iPhone, and a whole new category of IT products with the iPad. Steve Jobs built his company on passion, and today it's breaking boundaries and redefining whole new markets, while other players are scrambling to stay in the game through acquisitions.

"Apple at the core, its core value, is that we believe that people with passion can change the world for the better."

Steve Jobs, Motivational Speech after returning to Apple in 1997

Steve Jobs was brilliant at understanding what a product should be. According to Donald Norman, a former vice president for advanced technology at Apple, "Steve Jobs went to product reviews every week. He'd say, 'Move that two pixels over.' Then he'd come back a month later, and say, 'I told you to move that. Why didn't you?' That's a unique characteristic. He cared about details and he remembered." Steve Jobs was deeply passionate, and only because of this passion he was able to put in the required effort and to continuously challenge himself and his business in an effort to build something unique, functional, and beautiful.

But to be truly successful you need more than passion. You need to be able to pair passion with hard work and discipline, just as Steve Jobs did. Scientists have been producing remarkably consistent findings across a wide array of fields. These findings reveal that there is no substitute for discipline (Ericsson, 2006). People typically need around ten years of hard work before becoming outstanding. Moreover, the best people in any field are those who devote the most hours to practice; activity intended to improve performance to reach for higher levels of competence. The more you practice, the better your performance.

X-factor 2: Care for Customers

The restaurant La Parra de Burriana in Nerja, on the Spanish Costa del Sol thrives on tourist in the holiday period from May to October. In the rest of the year the locals should keep this restaurant afloat. What do you do then if a local expatriate community, the Donkey Sanctuary, holds their annual dinner in your restaurant? Obviously, you provide them with a great experience to build your reputation, and convince them to return, as their business can provide an important source of income in the low season. Instead, 26 year old Laurence Davy, owner of the restaurant, lets them wait for hours, only to present overcooked kebab and burned desserts. On top of this, he even dares to charge them dearly for such a dismal performance. No surprise then that the expats their tightly knit networks stay far away after such a shocking experience.

This behaviour of Laurence Davy is by no means unique. Many restaurant owners in Kitchen Nightmares show tremendous disrespect to their customers. This is a fatal mistake. In the restaurant business happy customers build reputations. If a customer had a very nice lunch, they will spread the word and by 5 p.m. people will be saying, "I'll go there for dinner because I had a great lunch." Of course, a welcoming atmosphere is important, but the quality of the food is absolutely critical. Provide good food and customers will remember you. They will come back.

"A business absolutely devoted to service will have only one worry about profits. They will be embarrassingly large."

Henry Ford

Nevertheless, our TV shows are chock-a-block with chefs who feel that the opinion of the customer does not add value. Andy, the owner and chef of le Bistro in sunny South Florida is such an example. Andy thinks he is perfect in every way. If customers send food back to him because it is raw or undercooked, Andy refuses to even look at the returned food, let alone taste it. He thinks he is always right and his food is perfect. Another example is Michel, the French chef of The Secret Garden in Moorpark, California. He says that the customer is 'almost' always right, although in practice he never agrees with any customer complaint. It is fair to say that Michel does not respond well to criticism. In the words of one of his waiters: "He's got an ego the size of France."

Care for customers means many things for a restaurant. For example, amongst others, it refers to the way you interact with customers, the level of service, cleanliness, the quality of the ingredients, and the quality of the food. Price is often an underestimated factor herein. Gordon Ramsay is especially tenacious in this respect. He explains, "You should ask an honest price for your services." So, you should not overprice your dishes, how tempting this might be. After all, how can you expect a customer to be satisfied and come back if you overcharge them? How can you really say you care for your customers if you in reality take advantage of them?

Interestingly enough, a vicious circle tends to develop with failing restaurants. Failing restaurants are often in dire need for funds and tend to increase their prices. Instead of earning more money, however, they in fact earn even less money because more and more customers feel they are taken advantage of. Not only will customers not return, they will also contribute to the negative reputation of the restaurant (i.e., they will tell their friends and family that the restaurant is too expensive or overprice; a phrase common heard from customers of the failing restaurants in Kitchen Nightmares). In such situations, one should be especially wary of banks and external accountants. They tend to give the advice to raise prices, which often is the straw that breaks the camel's back. Never forget that banks and accountants only care about money, and not about customers. The best answer in this respect can be summarized with another saying, let the cobbler stick to his last.

Needless to say, customer centric orientation is important in all businesses, not only in restaurants. In organizational science there is even a name for this, the service-profit chain (SPC). As Rucci, Kirn, and Quinn (1998: 84) note, "Any person with even a little experience … understands intuitively that there is a chain of cause and effect running from employee behaviour to customer behaviour to profits." This path runs from customer orientation via customer satisfaction and loyalty to financial performance. Strangely enough, the number of large businesses that are really capable of providing great service are rather limited. A business that does really well in terms of customer service is Zappos (see Zappos.com), the online retailer. They have a 100 percent satisfaction-guaranteed return policy, and the company will never fuss about any return. In fact, Zappos actually encourages customers to order several products, check them out, and return what they don't want. Incredible customer service is used to create an extremely loyal customer base. In the restaurant business, it works exactly the same, if you provide customers with a satisfying experience, they will definitely come back.

X-factor 3: Stand out from the Crowd

Moore Place is a restaurant located in a town called Esher in a very prosperous part of the Greater London Urban Area. In the past, the restaurant was always packed with customers, but bad service and bad food have driven customers away. New owners Richard and Mick have asked Gordon Ramsay to revamp their restaurant and get customers back in. To understand the nature and level of the competition Gordon walks through downtown Esher and sees a rich town with a lot of prosperous restaurants. It will not be easy to lure customers away from the competition and back to Moore Place. But Gordon discovers that a large US firm has their headquarters in Esher. Over 1000 Americans are living in the town, but there is not a single American restaurant. So, Gordon reinvents Moore Place by creating an American inspired menu with American classics such as clam chowder and great burgers. The burger instantaneously becomes Moore Place's signature dish, because it is a unique product that perfectly fits with the demand of its potential customers.

Gordon Ramsay shows that to run a successful restaurant, you have to understand the challenges and opportunities in its environment. What do your local customers value, and what are your competitors offering? You also have to be familiar with the local produce. What ingredients are available fresh, in abundance, and cheap? And, how can you use these ingredients to create a unique offering? Last but not least, what is unique to your place, and how will you persuade customers to visit and revisit your restaurant? In other words, what is the unique selling point or USP of the restaurant?

It is amazing how many small restaurants forget to take the competitive business environment into consideration. It is not uncommon that a starting entrepreneur opens a conventional Italian restaurant in a small town with already dozens of other Italian restaurants. Many inexperienced restaurateurs think that customers will come in, just by opening a new restaurant. This is hardly the case. To make sure that you use the environment to your advantage, you first have to understand the environment and the opportunities it presents. Next, you have to create an offering that makes optimal use of these opportunities. Finally you have to make sure that your unique offering is noticed by customers by marketing the restaurant. You have to think about the things that can make your restaurant new and unique, and that differentiates it from competitors.

For a restaurant to find a unique niche is basically a three-step process. First, you have to do a little research to understand the customers and the competition in your market.

You can get some information from your local Chamber of Commerce, but a simple stroll along the neighborhood can also do the trick. Is your restaurant set in a close net town where building a long-term reputation is key to success? Or is your restaurant set in a tourist town where visibility and location are crucial? What is the level of the competition? Are their many restaurants in your neighborhood? Which ones are doing great and what type of restaurant is currently lacking? Second, after forming a good understanding of the needs of your potential customers and the level of the competition, a restaurant owner should scrutinize his own restaurant. Which assets does the restaurant possesses that may be leveraged in the business environment? Does it have a great chef or maître-d? What is the quality of the location? Does the restaurant have loyal customers? Can you build on former glory? Third, in general, a restaurant should use fresh local produce. On the one hand, this fresh local produce virtually guarantees fresh local dishes. On the other hand, it attracts local people, who are proud of their local produce and value the local sourcing, as it contribute to the prosperity of the local community. If done properly, it also attracts people from outside the region, as the restaurant becomes the culinary ambassador of the region. It also makes economic sense, as the abundance of local produce implies low prices, as it virtually eliminates the costs of transportation. This kind of makes you wonder what Peter and Lois were thinking when they decided to offer Japanese and Kiwi meals at the Sandgate Hotel, which is situated at the English channel.

A nice example of how to effectively adapt a restaurant to its environment is provided by the episode on Momma Cherri's Soul Food Shack. The restaurant is located in Brighton, England, a touristic seaside city. This is an environment that is characterized by seasonal and cyclical patterns, which demands creative solutions. Gordon correctly observes that the restaurant basically has two different markets, a small local market during low season (i.e., winter months and weekdays) and a sizeable tourist market during high season (i.e., summer months and weekends). Hence, Gordon decides to create a ten pound three-course meal for weekdays (i.e., low season), and a larger menu with more expensive meals for the weekend (i.e., high season). These two separate menus are a creative adaptive solution to overcome the problem of seasonal and cyclical patterns in the restaurant business.

Another example of using your unique strengths can be found in the episode on The Curry Lounge. This Indian restaurant in Nottingham, England is plagued by severe competition with more than 18 Indian restaurants in a single mile radius. The restaurant owner, ex-sales director Raz, tries to stand out from the crowd by untruthfulness (e.g., he advertises that the Curry Lounge is the best Indian restaurant, which it is clearly not), awkward interior design, and a kind of Do-It-Yourself (DIY) menu where customers can assemble their own combinations of Indian food. This DIY menu does not only cause severe problems for the kitchen, but also leads to extensive customer confusion. Gordon decides to reinvent the menu based on strengths of Rhakir Khan, a chef from the northern mountainous part of India, with ample experience in traditional Indian cooking. To continue with the traditional theme, Gordon also decides to add so-called Tiffin-boxes to the menu, which are authentic Indian lunchboxes that hold bread (or naan), curry, and rice. The Tiffin-boxes are sold to nearby businesses for a mere five pounds each. This not only increases revenues and profits in a direct way, but also allows potential customers to become acquainted with the authentic Indian kitchen of The Curry Lounge, and convince them to visit the restaurant in the evening or during the weekend. By combining the authentic North-Indian menu with Tiffin-boxes, The Curry Lounge is able to distinguish itself apart from its competition.

All these examples illustrate the fact that it is important to find a unique selling point, which appeals to customers and sets your restaurant apart from its competitors. This different angle may be based on the characteristics of the environment and location, but a proposition is often much stronger and harder to copy if it is based on the unique capabilities of owner and staff.

Success comes from knowing that you did your best to become the best that you are capable of becoming.

John Wooden

Knowing what you can and cannot be best at is the root of all business strategy. In his book, Jim Collins (2001) explains the story of Abbot Laboratories. In the 1960s, Abbott Laboratories and Upjohn were virtually indistinguishable, when they decided to go their separate routes. Abbott Laboratories concluded the sad reality that it had already lost the game of becoming the largest pharmaceutical company in the world, because it would not be able to catch up with the huge research lead of big pharmaceutical companies like Merck. Abbott Laboratories CEO, George Cain, therefore dared to ask the one and only logical question, "What can we be best at?" Abbott Laboratories concluded that it could be unique in creating products that provided cost-effective health care, and the company began to move toward being number one in this domain. At the same time, Upjohn was still trying to beat Merck. Unfortunately, they had a hard lesson to learn: just because something is your core business doesn't mean you can be the best at it! After fighting this losing R&D battle, Upjohn saw its profits dwindle, and was finally acquired in 1995 by Pharmacia. Abbot Laboratories, on the contrary, showed great returns throughout the following decades.

X-factor 4: Ingenuity in Marketing

Oscar's is an Irish family-run restaurant in the heart of the beautiful English countryside. Unfortunately, however, it is located above a butcher's shop, and second-floor establishments are notoriously difficult to fill. The reason is that such restaurants are not be easily noticed by people who are passing by. Due to tight budgets, Gordon does not want to spend serious money on advertising in the local newspaper to attract customers. Instead, he decides to explore a more creative, cheaper, and more permanent solution. Gordon talks to the butcher below, and proposes to establish a partnership between the restaurant and the butcher. This partnership implies that the butcher will be the exclusive supplier of meat to the restaurant. In return, the butcher is asked to install blinds for his windows that are to be lowered after the butcher closes, which informs passersby that Oscar's is located above the butcher on the second floor. Furthermore, the menu of the restaurant also mentions the exclusive relationship with the butcher below. This way, Gordon has constructed a win-win for Oscar's and the butcher. The butcher wholeheartedly agrees. This example shows that ingenuity is often much more important for marketing than money.

A similar example is found in the episode on The Glass House. This restaurant is located in Ambleside, a small but touristic town in Cumbria, North West England. The restaurant is set just outside the town center, and is pretty hard to spot. The restaurant is hidden in the scenery, and has no visible sign to attract customers. Therefore, Gordon decides to create a beautiful sign with a menu, which is visible to passing customers, and naturally blends into the environment. The sign is almost like a work of art, and grabs the attention of tourists in a subtle way. As such, it attracts curious customers to the restaurant. This is another example that shows that creative thinking goes a lot further than standard marketing. As a general rule, an entrepreneur should find creative ways to get attention. After all, marketing does not have to be expensive and can go much further than local ads in the newspaper and a local commercial on the radio.

Another low-cost method to promote an ailing restaurant is to organize an event to create a so-called 'buzz' in the local community. This technique can be used in various forms. For instance, in Dillon's (later renamed Purnima), an Indian restaurant in Manhattan, New York City, Gordon organizes some sort of parade. The parade includes a hop-on hop-off bus with Indian music, traditionally dressed and beautiful Indian dancers, and free Indian food. In this way, Gordon attracts attention to the relaunch of Purnima, and creates a 'buzz' in the local community that will attract customers. Handing out free food (i.e., giveaways or free trials) is a well-known marketing method that is extremely effective, and can also be easily applied in the restaurant business. It does not always have to be as grand as the parade to relaunch Purnima. For example, at Momma Cherri's, Gordon takes Charita to the beach with a BBQ, to have her cook live for people that are passing by to promote Charita's cooking and the restaurant. This worked miracles, as the reservations are pouring in for the next days. Charita takes this lesson to heart, and organizes a fourth of July celebration with live music and BBQ each year. After all, a happy event with free and tasty food is almost always a great way to lure people into a restaurant.

Perhaps one of the nicest examples of creating a buzz in the community is the campaign for real gravy. Inspired by Gordon, who wondered why traditional English gravy has disappeared in English pubs, Brian and his wife Elaine, the owners of The Fenwick Arms, started a campaign for real gravy. According to Brian and Elaine, they rediscovered traditional gravy and now want to drive people back to use the juices from roasts again. This campaign was so successful that it went far beyond a local event, and increased the reputation and recognition of the pub nationwide with over 5 million followers.

Gordon Ramsay's approach to marketing can best be compared to guerrilla marketing techniques where marketing campaigns are unconventional and consumers are targeted in unexpected places in order to generate a buzz (Levinson, 1998). It is based on human psychology and instead of money, the primary investment is time, energy, and imagination. The goal is a positive "buzz" around the restaurant. According to Gordon, "business does not come and sit on your lap, you have to look for it and find it." Gordon's marketing campaigns are positive, funny, and always firmly strengthen the new identity of the restaurant. For instance, in the case of The Granary, where the old restaurant was considered to be too posh, Gordon decided to re-launch the restaurant with a food fair day, especially designed for families with young children. To further strip the restaurant from its posh image, Gordon had the owner walking around in a chicken suit to entertain the guests and children.

In marketing, you must choose between boredom, shouting, and seduction. Which do you prefer?

Roy H. Williams

While guerilla marketing is especially popular amongst Small or Medium Enterprises (SMEs), who do not have a multimillion dollar advertising budget to work with, large multinationals are also increasingly turning to more creative forms of marketing. The reason is that many people have become averse to polished, professional ads and more creative and original approaches to marketing are needed to attract positive attention. A remarkable example of a low-cost marketing effort with enormous impact outside the restaurant business can be found in Paris, France. Here, Médecins du Monde (i.e., doctors of the world), a global humanitarian organization, have been organizing activities to draw attention to the issue of homelessness in Paris since 1993. In 2005, they cleverly decided to distribute 300 tents that carried the logo of the Médecins du Monde to vagabonds in Paris. Suddenly, hundreds of homeless tents were set up in Paris, mostly along the beautiful Parisian canals, hereby bringing a great deal of media attention to the issue of homelessness. It provoked such a commotion that the mayor of Paris was forced to do something, and almost immediately the French government allocated nearly $10 million for emergency housing in Paris to create 1,270 hostel beds.

X-factor 5: Every Ship needs a Captain

D-place is a trendy fusion restaurant in Essex owned by Mexican immigrant, Israel. When the restaurant first opened, it was a huge success, and Israel quickly decided to open more restaurants in an effort to build a small empire. However, despite his initial fortunes, Israel's luck changed, and he needed to shut all but one of his restaurants. Now, D-place is the only restaurant left in his empire, and it is not doing very well either. If the restaurant goes under, Israel and his wife Tara would be ruined by the half-million pound debt they owe the brewery. It is crucially important for Israel that D-place will be successful again. The restaurant is more confusion than fusion. There is torturous treatment of innocent food and bad service. On top of all this, chef Philippe and restaurant manager Dave are in constant battle. To get the restaurant afloat again, this has to stop and it is Israel's role to stop it. However, Israel hesitates to intervene, and appreciates his role as a boss too little and too late. In the end, he loses the restaurant and he and his wife retain their massive debt.

Every ship needs a captain, and every business a leader. Obviously, this starts at the top of the hierarchy, with the owner of the restaurant (or business). Much like the captain on a ship, the role of the owner is to provide direction to the restaurant and guarantee its smooth functioning, by putting the right person in the right place, telling them explicitly what is required of them, and controlling the quality of the food and service, hereby making sure that customers are satisfied and the restaurant prospers. Just like a captain cannot sail a ship alone, the owner of a restaurant cannot run the restaurant all by himself, and he needs to employ others to get the job done. As explained in the introduction, the head chef stands at the helm of the kitchen, and the maître-d at the helm of the dining room. The proper functioning of any restaurant not only requires that the captain's two lieutenants (head chef and maître-d) provide the proper leadership and guidance to their employees, but also that the lieutenants communicate, coordinate, and cooperate to ensure the smooth functioning of the restaurant as a whole.

"If the head chef and general manager get along, then everybody will follow suit."

Gordon Ramsay

When the captain is not able to set the proper direction and provide guidance to the lieutenants, mutiny follows, the quality of food and service deteriorates, and customers are disappointed. This is clearly illustrated in the above example of D-place where, due to the lack of leadership from the owner, the head chef and the maître-d fight for dominance. This ultimately results in a breakdown of communication, inconsistent food, and a service that is seriously below par. Consequently, customers are disappointed, seats remain empty, and the end is very near. Lack of leadership is perhaps the primary cause of failing restaurants. Due to the lack of guidance, employees start doing as they please, paying little attention to the quality of service, which is required to prevent the ship from sinking altogether.

Another interesting case in point is The Mixing Bowl in Bellmore, New York, where Billy is also the chef of the restaurant and runs the kitchen. He trusts Mike, the general manager, to run the front of house. But Mike is doing a lousy job and Billy is not managing Mike. So the restaurant keeps struggling during the whole turnaround. At the end of the show Gordon tells Billy, "Billy, I am brutally honest. You need a manager and Mike is not your man." Even then Billy does not sack Mike. Billy's example is by no means unique. A weak owner is probably one of the most frequent and hardest problems to resolve, and not only in the restaurant business. In all TV-shows on turnaround management, involving all countries, you find owners who are reluctant to make difficult decisions leading to failing or struggling businesses.

Any restaurant that wants to be successful needs to have strong leadership. While the absence of a leader is one scenario that often leads to failure, the presence of multiple leaders may also lead to the collapse of the business. For example, at Morgan's, a restaurant in a blooming area of Liverpool, there are three captains at the helm, and they cannot decide who is in charge. This sends out inconsistent messages to restaurant staff, as they do not know who to listen to. The message that the leaders give is one of conflict, struggle, and indecisiveness. It is logical that this leads to inconsistent, low quality food combined with dismal service, which left customers awfully disappointed. Gordon takes the three women (Sandy, Helen, and Laura) to the playground (a moral lesson as they are acting like children) and asks each of them what their role and tasks are. Nobody knows and everybody disagrees. He tells the ladies, "Nobody runs it, if you are not prepared to take the responsibility." In the end Gordon appoints Helen to be general manager, to the disappointment and shock of sister Laura and mother Sandy.

My main job was developing talent. I was a gardener providing water and other nourishment to our top 750 people. Of course, I had to pull out some weeds, too.

Jack Welch

One of the greatest and most well-known business leaders of the last 25 years is probably Jack Welch, former CEO of General Electric (between 1981-2001). Much has been said about how Welch transformed the American industrial giant. Welch has reshaped the company through more than 600 acquisitions and an ambitious expansion strategy. Jack Welch was able to wield power and influence over a business empire spanning 100 countries and employing approximately 300,000 employees. His behaviour has been well documented and it goes beyond the scope of this chapter to discuss all his qualities. However, he attributes his success to three simple themes: focus, execution, and people. From his biography, entitled "Jack: Straight from the gut" (Welch and Byrne, 2008), you can learn how much time he spends on people and building a leadership team. Selecting the right people, training people, listening to people, and giving talents new opportunities were possibly his finest levers. These levers all aimed to create the strongest possible leadership team. Jack Welch understood that a great leadership team is crucial for success in any business. In the restaurant business, this is the alignment of three key players: owner, chef and maître-d.

X-factor 6: Focus on the Negatives

Down city is a restaurant in Providence, Rhode Island that is run by co-owner Abby. When Gordon first arrives on the scene, he asks Abby how she rates the food in the restaurant. She claims that the food is a perfect 10. After tasting the food, amongst others a so-called "Award Winning Meatloaf," Gordon Ramsay bluntly tells her that the food is shockingly bad and embarrassing. To the staff and co-owner Rico, this is no surprise at all, as they have been trying to tell Abby for years now. Abby, however, does not agree at all, and tells Gordon, "I think you are one of those customers that I would fire immediately." Gordon asks in amazement, "You fire customers?"

At first glance, the behaviour of Abby in the scene seems completely absurd and illogical. How can you refute the opinion of your customers, staff, and co-owner for years? Even worse, where does she get the idea of actually starting an argument about the quality of food with a world-renowned chef who has earned many Michelin stars? It is actually quite logical that the owner of a failing restaurant is in denial. After all, to own a failing restaurant implies not seeing what is actually wrong with the restaurant. Otherwise, the restaurant wouldn't be failing, as you would simply change whatever is wrong with the restaurant. The reason why many owners are in denial is because their personal identity and self-image are closely tied to the restaurant, and its success. To protect their identity and self-image, they need to maintain the image that the restaurant is successful, and thus invalidate all negative feedback that claims otherwise. According to their opinion, negative feedback is simply not allowed to be true, and they need to come up with other reasons why Gordon (or anyone else, for that matter) would say negative things about the restaurant (and by extension, them).

There are also less severe examples of denial. For example, in The Runaway Girl, a restaurant in Sheffield, England, owner Justin does not bluntly deny negative news, but carefully filters it. He simply pays less attention to negative news and emphasizes any positive feedback. Because he wants positive feedback from his customers, he asks suggestive questions that encourage positive feedback. When Justin is once again fishing for compliments from customers, Gordon bluntly tells him, "Stop massaging yourself." Justin's behaviour to deny negative news is quite common, as most owners and chefs in Kitchen Nightmares report that they do not understand why customers stay away. These owners and chefs usually report that the food is good and customers leave happy. Actual negative comments of customers are denied far beyond the belief of the neutral spectator. For example, in Morgan's, the family owned restaurant in Liverpool, one of the sisters comments about a customer who is waiting for over an hour, "He is quite happy to wait."

These scenes illustrate why it is important to focus on the negatives. First, this prevents that people's self-image is tied to the restaurant, and that personal egos do not become over-inflated. Second, by focusing on the negatives, the owner's attention is directed towards what needs to be improved. After all, without negatives, there is no room for improvement. In the words of Gordon Ramsay, "My chefs only want to know what is wrong, not what's right." Third, it forces the owner to be honest, both to his or her customers and staff by genuinely asking what is wrong with the restaurant. As an owner, you should be inquisitive and address the negativities as they arise. For example, when food is returned, taste it yourself, so that you know what is wrong. Gordon explains to Justin of The Runaway Girl, "Admitting your mistakes and saying where you were wrong as a restaurateur is the first step of turning things around."

There is no failure. Only feedback.

Robert Allen

The tendency to focus on the positives and disregard the negatives is fundamentally human. It is a natural part of human nature and closely related to the survival instinct. Consider these phrases: turning a blind eye, burying your head in the sand, ignorance is bliss, and living a lie. These are a few examples of well-known phrases, which show how common denial is. The most obvious form of denial is when someone denies a fact altogether (either because they don't know, they block it out, or they choose to ignore it altogether). Abby demonstrates this when she disagrees with Gordon's assessment of the food quality. She simply dismisses the fact and states that it is not true. We will see in later chapters that it is difficult to break through severe and even moderate forms of denial. Barring a very, very serious crisis, people tend to prefer the comfort of denial.

In his recent book, Robert Tedlow (2010) lists many examples in history where big organizations failed by discarding negative information. One of his examples is Henry Ford, who firmly believed that consumers would continue to want black cars, in the face of many contrary signals. The author explains that all once-great companies that have fallen from grace appear to have one persistent belief, "If you simply avoid speaking the truth, all the problems will just go away." While an obvious fallacy, many companies seem to fall into this trap. A well-known example is Sears Roebuck and Co (i.e., Sears). The story starts in 1973, when Sears moved into the world's tallest building, the 110-story Sears Tower in Chicago. At that same time, an elegant gentleman and old-fashioned businessman, called Arthur Wood, takes chair of the company. With him also enters the conviction that the retail market is saturated, and that the only way forward is to enter new lines of business, such as financial brokering. How it is possible, in 1973, that Sears is convinced that its market is saturated remains a mystery until today. After all, in this day-and-age, there are still fortunes to be made in retailing, as demonstrated by Wal-Mart's spectacular success in the 1970s and 1980s. Instead, at Sears, executives were trying to convince themselves they would success selling "socks and stocks." This strategy of unrelated diversification burned lots of hard-earned cash, and Sears, despite divesture efforts in the 1990s, never fully recovered. In early 2005, Sears was acquired by Kmart. At that time, its lofty tower was already abandoned, as it was already sold in 1994, after being largely vacant for more than a decade.

X-factor 7: Teamwork

Neill is the owner of The Granary, a restaurant in Titchfield, England. He has invited the front of house team for a friendly get together in a pub, but he purposely did not invite the kitchen team to this meeting. What message does this give to your chefs? A message of belonging or togetherness? Hardly. No wonder that Gordon becomes furious with Neill, and explains, "The buck stops with the boss ... there is no way he is getting away with this." According to Gordon Ramsay, the kitchen and the front-of-house are part of one big family. There is no room for hidden agendas, secret meetings, factions, and islands. Such things will only lead to fragmentation and conflict, which prevents the smooth functioning of the restaurant as a whole. Great teamwork and communication are crucial in the restaurant business, where a variety of skills are needed to make the place a success and where stress is a basic ingredient. There is no single person who can make a restaurant successful singlehandedly and there is limited room for error. In reality, we see many restaurants with failing teams. Creating and maintaining a performing team is not easy and requires a good understanding of people and social processes. Furthermore, you need to continually invest in the team. For this reason, Gordon states that he has an outing with his restaurant staff at least once a month, in order to bond with people while creating mutual understanding and acceptance.

A restaurant thrives on teamwork and three ingredients are important. The first ingredient is a shared objective (Bottom-Left in Figure 9); i.e., why are we doing the things we do? All team members strive to accomplish the same thing (e.g., the restaurant is financially successful or has a great gastronomical reputation). Without the willingness to accomplish the same objective, the team fragments with hidden agendas, which provides the basis for conflict, failure, and disappointment. An obvious example is fragmented ownership, where owners have different strategies for the restaurant, such as the NYC restaurant Black Pearl, where the three owners (i.e., Brian, Greg, and David) do not see eye-to-eye and have completely different visions on the direction of the restaurant. No wonder the staff asks the simple question, "Why don't we have *one* general manager?"

The second ingredient of teamwork is structure or the definition of tasks (Top-Left in Figure 9). This implies asking the question: who does what? The restaurant needs to be structured in such a way to maximize the likelihood of achieving the shared objective. This relates to defining clear roles and responsibilities. Fuzzy roles and responsibilities are a recipe for disaster, by creating the opportunity to deny responsibility and do as little as possible. A telling sign of fuzzy responsibilities is an overdose of 'managers'.

For example, in The Sandgate Hotel, even Gordon gets confused by the division of labor between the general manager, the food and beverages manager, and the restaurant manager. He explains, "It is like a jigsaw, where none of the pieces really fit." In Dillon's in New York City a similar picture emerges. There is a general manager, an operational manager, and a floor manager. To add to the confusion, Andrew, the operational manager, sometimes cooks meals in the restaurant.

Clarity of roles not only lets you know who is responsible for doing what, but also enables performance management, as it helps to determine who is doing a good job, and who is not. In Morgan's, a restaurant in a trendy Liverpool neighborhood, Gordon says to the owners: "I want you to let your chef do his job, and if he doesn't do his job, get rid of him." It is as simple as that. Clarity of roles prevents people from taking over activities from others. To take responsibility for someone else's role generally leads to confusion within the team and tends to result in failure. This is especially true when the person does not possess the necessary skills, which is what we observed within The Walnut Tree Inn, Wales. Here Francesco, a trained and distinguished Maître-d, has bought a famous countryside Michelin star restaurant. But, when the head-chef departs, Francesco is left with an enormous problem, as it is difficult to find a quality chef in rural Wales. Sadly, though, Francesco does not trust the skills of the remaining chefs in the kitchen. Francisco decides to take the role of chef himself. He explains, "I can only be the one." However, Francisco is not a great chef. Moreover, he has great capabilities as a Maître-d, and excels at selling expensive wines that compliment the food. By taking the role of chef, Francesco basically accomplishes four things. First, he reduces food quality because he lacks the appropriate culinary skills. Second, customer service deteriorates, as Francesco's capabilities are missed front-of-house. Third, sales of expensive wine decline. Finally, Francisco's leadership is undermined, as he attempts to fulfill multiple roles.

The final ingredient of teamwork is clear and unambiguous operational processes (Top-Right in Figure 9). This last ingredient concerns how team members perform their tasks and how they interact with each other. Restaurant staff needs to work together like a well-oiled machine to ensure evening service runs smoothly.

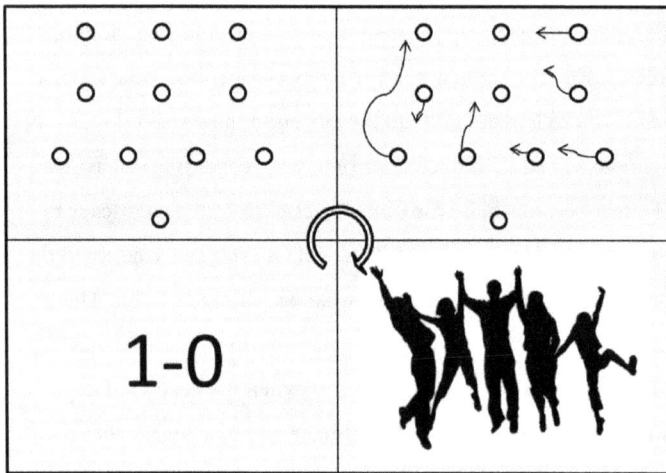

Figure 9 The three ingredients of teamwork: why, what, and how

Whether a restaurant functions as a team can often be determined by watching a picture or video of the restaurant staff. If everybody in this picture is really smiling and enjoying themselves, this usually means that everything is fine (Bottom-Right in Figure 9).

Individuals play the game, but teams beat the odds.

SEAL Team saying

Although teamwork, effective teams, and team building are well-researched topics in today's organizations, it is still hard to find commercial businesses that excel in teamwork. Most of our institutions and companies remain founded on the idea of individual merit. Perhaps the best examples of teamwork are found in the armed forces where soldiers often operate in volatile, uncertain, complex, and ambiguous environments (a.k.a., VUCA-environments). To work effectively in such a setting, individuals collaborate intensively to comprehend the various signals of this constantly changing environment. No single person can survive on his or her own in such an environment. It takes an effective and cooperative team to solve the variety of problems one encounters in battle.

In light of the above, teamwork is of tremendous importance within a restaurant. After all, during service, a restaurant bears many of the characteristics found in a VUCA environment.

X-factor 8: Keep It Simple Stupid

The Curry Lounge is an Indian restaurant in Nottingham, England and loses over £3000 a week. The major problem of the restaurant is blatantly obvious. The major problem facing this restaurant is a complicated menu offering about a hundred variations of curry. In an effort to cater for every individual customer taste, owner Raz has invented an overly complex DIY-style menu. In allowing customers to create individual combinations, he effectively discards thousands of years of experience associated with Indian food. Because customers are inexperienced they combine flavors that to not match, which results in disappointment and a constant stream of complaints to front-of-house staff, who subsequently blame the kitchen staff. Although Raz actually believes he is meeting customer demand, he is not. This results in enormous pressure on all staff, and a chef who is close to losing his mind.

A golden rule among restaurateurs is simplicity. This rule applies to all aspects of running a restaurant including the menu, dishes, processes, roles and responsibilities. In Gordon's words, "the basic model of any successful restaurant is the same everywhere, [...] fresh ingredients, simply cooked, [...] it is not rocket science." For a restaurant to be successful, it is important that all aspects of the restaurant are streamlined and operate to accomplish a shared objective. During lunch and dinner service, restaurants are characterized by periods of extreme pressure as customers expect high quality products and services delivered almost instantaneously. In order to accomplish this task, all aspects of the restaurant need to be straightforward, so that the restaurant can function like a well-oiled machine. This involves a simple menu, dishes that can be easily prepared, clear-cut procedures with well-defined roles and responsibilities that facilitate communication, coordination, and cooperation between the kitchen and dining room. This approach should allow staff to deal with the extreme pressures of service while delivering customer satisfaction.

Adding complexity to this interdependent chain, results in an inability to effectively manage a busy service. Instead of achieving a natural 'flow', pressure builds up somewhere in process, and eventually breaks down all effective communication, coordination, and cooperation. Overly complex menus place a heavy strain on all aspects of the restaurant. As customer orders become more complex, they are more difficult to remember by the staff, which increases the likelihood of mistakes. From a chef's perspective, increased complexity results in a complicated cooking process because a wide variety of dishes reduce the chef's ability to achieve cooking perfection. This has the knock-on effect of reducing delivery of quality dishes to tables at the same time. This is illustrated by a simple mathematical rule. When increasing the number of items that can be combined linearly, the number of potential recombinations increases exponentially (Carroll and Hannan, 2000). Hence, the process of coordinating all possible dish combination becomes extremely complex. Furthermore, purchasing and procurement also becomes much more of a challenge, because increasing the number of ingredients implies a slower turnover of individual ingredients (i.e., it takes longer to finish individual ingredients). This will increase the time ingredients spend in the restaurant and will make it more difficult to maintain the freshness of ingredients, which is the cardinal rule of cooking. Before you know it, chefs start freezing ingredients and pre-cooked dishes, to prevent the ingredients from going off and to be able to manage cooking several dishes while managing a small team.

In many failing restaurants, the trouble starts with overly complicated menus. For example, The Fish and Anchor, Lampeter, Wales is run by ex-boxer Mike and his wife Caron. Mike won 700,000 pounds and bought his Michelin star dream by acquiring the Fish and Anchor. With the help of dozens of home cookbooks, he tries to to cook as a professional chef, but it is an uphill battle as he is no trained as a chef and home recipes are way too complicated to be cooked efficiently in any restaurant. In the end his home cooked recipes lead to an unbearable situation where less than 50 percent of customers are served and tensions mounts between kitchen and service staff.

In several episodes, Gordon simplifies of the menu, dishes, and processes in the restaurant. Not only does this make everybody's job easier, but also clarifies the message sent to the customers. Instead of being confused by a complex menu, a simple menu sends out a clear, concise message that can be easily understood by the customers.

Make things as simple as possible, but not simpler.

Albert Einstein

A classic example of the power of simplification happened at Apple when Steve Jobs returned after 11 years of absence. Given Apple's dire situation (near bankruptcy), Steve Jobs was desperate to cut costs and, at the same time, create new products to boost profits and cash flow. To increase his understanding of what Apple had been doing in terms of innovation, he invited his R&D department to evaluate what kind of projects they had been working on and to get a grasp on the quality of Apple's pipeline of inventions. He quickly discovered that Apple had over 3000 different R&D initiatives. During a meeting where the R&D teams explained the different projects, Steve Jobs walked to the whiteboard and drew a 2-by-2 matrix with four cells. One axe of the matrix displayed PC vs. laptop, the other axe displayed professional vs. consumer market. Then Steve said: "I only want four projects, one PC for the consumer market, one PC for the professional market, a laptop for the consumer market, and finally a laptop for the professional market. Four projects to make four great products." In a masterstroke 3000 projects were simplified to four central endeavors that together proved to be the foundation of Apple's recovery in the 1990's.

X-factor 9: Quality Control

Fiesta Sunrise is a family-run Mexican eatery in West Nyack, New York. As usual, the owner is in complete denial. The financial situation of the restaurant is deteriorating, because of a lack of customers, who decide to stay away from the old and greasy food. The kitchen is infested with insects and cockroaches, and there are enough cooked beans to feed an army. Gordon confronts owner Vic with the situation, and explains that he is "overstaffed, overstocked, and underworked." Of course, Vic disagrees. Fed up with his complete and utter indifference, Gordon challenges Vic to take out one of the disgusting containers of greasy beans and show them to the customers. While Vic refuses, Gordon does not hesitate, and takes the beans into the restaurant, plants them on the table, and announces to everyone that this is where the food they are consuming originates. Gordon then addresses one of the customers, "Sir, that thing in your hand, put it down, if you would have seen where it comes from, you wouldn't be eating it." Gordon apologizes to the customers and informs them that the restaurant is being shut down for the day.

While quality is multidimensional, the most important dimension of quality is basic hygiene. When working with food, hygiene is of the utmost importance, because not living up to health standards can lead to severe health problems of customers, and will unavoidably lead to the immediate closure of even the most profitable business. Understandably, hygiene is the also the first principle of cooking taught at every cooking school in this world. With respect to hygiene, there are six basic rules:

- Keep a spotless kitchen by cleaning after every service (i.e., lunch and dinner);
- Use fresh ingredients (and certainly not rotten);
- Label all food placed in the fridge (i.e., what is it and when was it cooked and placed in the fridge);
- Do not put raw and cooked meat together (to prevent cross-contamination);
- Do not put hot or warm food in the fridge (otherwise, bacteria will go to center and start breeding there);
- Taste the food (to make sure it meets the quality required; only way to maintain control and keep up standards).

Such basic rules of hygiene are taught at every cooking school and culinary college. So why is it then that so many of the failing restaurants forget these rules and are downright dirty? For example, at Dillon's, a restaurant in New York City, the flies are everywhere, and there are rats and cockroaches in the kitchen. At the Spanish Pavilion, an inspection of the freezer reveals stacks of unlabeled frozen food, and nobody knows how old these piles of food are. Gordon also finds bags of raw chicken, unlabeled and dripping with blood, that smell horrific. On top of that, there is even a pigeon flying in the kitchen. At PJ's Steakhouse, Gordon discovers loads of rotten fruit and vegetables in the storage, and at Classic American, the chef even tries to send out a dish with bad broccoli, which leads Gordon to decide to close down the kitchen for the rest of the day. Furthermore, at Grasshopper Also, Gordon finds cooked meat that is stored next to raw meat, and mozzarella sticks that are covered in blood. That this is no exception is showed in the Hannah and Mason's restaurant where they put cooked and raw chicken together!? At The Priory, they wrap things while still being warm that causes bacteria to grow, while at La Parra de Burriana, the chef is reheating yesterday's meat on the barbeque, and Gordon finds dog shit in the dining area. The list of unhygienic kitchens seems to go on and on and reads as a compilation of dead rats, live mice, and cockroaches. Regrettably, hygiene problems are not only limited to the preparation and storage of food. There are plenty of restaurants that demonstrate a complete disregard to sanitation. For example, in Californian restaurant Casa Roma, Gordon finds toilets covered in bodily fluids, and in the episode on Santé La Brea, a waiter covered in sweat stains is touching people all the time.

This lack of hygiene can largely be explained by one of the following reasons: (1) by a loss of passion, (2) by the laziness of both owners and chefs, and, sometimes (3) by a lack of funds. Nevertheless, there can never be an excuse for running a dirty unhygienic restaurant, which points to severe behavioural problems. Most restaurants do not start out with rotten ingredients, and it takes a while before chefs let standards slip to such an extent that it actually becomes a health hazard. However, it all starts with a lack of proper quality control that leads to a deterioration of standards. Therefore, quality control is extremely important in the restaurant business, and there is absolutely no excuse to let standards slip, no matter what the circumstances. This is precisely the reason why Gordon is so strict on standards and places so much importance on quality control.

Obviously, quality refers to other things besides hygiene. A restaurant should be a pleasurable to go to. A fine dining restaurant should lure people into staying somewhat longer, so they drink some extra wine and order a nice desert. No wonder then that a restaurant with a "Sunday church atmosphere" such as La Riviera in Inverness, Scotland has trouble keeping the business afloat. Dining is an experience that should satisfy all our senses, and besides taste, sight, smell, feeling, and hearing are also of extreme importance. Hence, a restaurant should avoid driving customers insane with an annoying intercom (The Sandgate Hotel), staring waiters (Rococo's), or a fighting couple (The Fish and Anchor).

To create a welcoming feeling, a restaurant has to mix a warm, relaxing interior with friendly and hospitable staff. This seems obvious to many of us, but so many restaurants make essential blunders. They either are too formal, like the funeral atmosphere in Fenwick Arms, or too informal, like the careless climate at the Sandgate Hotel, where waiter cannot be bothered by customers. One of the biggest and most common mistakes is probably that restaurant owners do not really care about his/her customer. The interior is almost never chosen in order to please the customer, but based on personal likes and dislikes of the owner. For example, Allan Love of Ruby Tate's restaurant in Brighton provides a nice case in point. The place looks like a night-club. On the wall there is modern art with spray-painted women's underpants, which, some would argue, is not particularly appetizing in a restaurant. When Gordon tries to change the décor, Allen Love, the owner, is furious. He is afraid that without these paintings the decor does not reflect his personality. He fails to realise that the interior is not there to please the owner, but the customer.

Quality is remembered long after the price is forgotten.

Gucci Family Slogan

While quality control is obvious in food (i.e., due to the associated health hazards), it is also of tremendous importance in other businesses. Proper control and testing can guarantee a certain minimum level of product and service quality, and a lack of quality control can lead to severe financial and reputation risks. Recently, in the pharmaceutical industry, Johnson & Johnson received reprimands from customers and the Federal Drug Administration (FDA) for its lack of quality control. Consumers complained that many of their products had "musty smells" after opening. In response to this critique the company recalled certain bottles of Motrin, Tylenol, Benadryl, and Zyrtec. The FDA reported that the manufacturing plant had a large gap in the ceiling, which lead to contamination of the product. The resulting shutdown of the plant has cost the company over $900 million in lost sales, while the loss of reputation will prove the most costly to this industry giant. Johnson and Johnsons is not alone. Several industry giants have also fallen foul of inadequate quality control. For example, Toyota was forced to recall tens of thousands of cars due to a break down in the quality control process.

X-factor 10: Business First

Classic American was bought a little bit over 10-years ago by Colleen and Naomi, two waitresses who already worked there at that time. Initially, the place was packed and business was booming. At this moment, however, the restaurant is dealing with crappy food, a debt of approximately $1 million, and a staff that does not care. The owners are way too friendly and treat their staff as family. To find the core problem of the restaurant, Gordon holds an anonymous question round. One of the questions to Naomi (one of the owners) is why she is such a push over. Naomi answers, "Because they are my family." Gordon disagrees, and explains, "They are not, your family is at home, this is your business." Gordon is very clear to Naomi, "There is no friendship, after the place closes, they leave and you are left with the debt."

Many restaurateurs want to be friends with their staff, at the cost of slipping standards, huge debts, and impending doom. For example, at La Lanterna, the owner and maître-d are close friends, but act like little boys while the restaurant fails. At Piccolo Teatro, owner Rachel has appointed her friend Stephanie, who couldn't care less about the problems Rachel faces, and is not really willing to put in any effort to turn the place around. In fact, when Gordon confronts her about this attitude, she gets upset and leaves, despite her supposed friendship with Rachel. At Momma Cherri's Soul Food Shack, Charita treats her staff as family, and they are not pulling their weight. Gordon explains to Charita that she has to get rid of the excess baggage and that she needs to "crack the whip," as kitchen staff has to be professional, which implies, "no smiling, no laughing, and serious work."

Effective management becomes impossible when you do not separate business and friendship. In The Sandgate Hotel, after diner service, staff was allowed to drink in the hotel bar. The staff brought in over 2000 pounds a month and the hotel became by and large dependent on this income. But as a result the relationship between management and staff gradually changed. The staff started to see themselves as customers, taking precedence over real customers, paid no attention to management, while effectively undermining the hierarchical relationship between management and staff.

A restaurant is a business, and should be treated as such. This means that anyone wanting to own a restaurant needs to have what it takes to be a leader, and stand above his or her staff, let them know what is required from them, correct when necessary, and get rid of any excess baggage. If not, standards will deteriorate, people will not take any responsibility, and the restaurant will head for disaster. The business is there to take care of the owner, not the other way round.

Being a professional leader of a restaurant can be very hard when working with friends and family. It is perhaps no coincidence that a lot of the failing restaurants in the TV-series are family run (but it is possible that the most profitable businesses could be family run). Some examples of badly managed family run restaurants from Kitchen Nightmares are Oscar's (run by mother and son), Morgan's (run by a mother and two daughters), The Sandgate Hotel (husband and wife), The Dovecote Bistro (father, mother, and daughter), Peter's (father, son, and daughter), Seascape (mother and son), Hot Potato Café (two sisters, and a sister-in-law), and Finn McCool's (a father with two sons). Buddy, the owner of Finn McCool, a restaurant in the Hamptons in New York is perhaps most clear about the difficulties of running a family restaurant when he states, "If Brian wasn't my son, I would have fired him."

A restaurant needs to be run like a business, with sound financials and cash flow. For example, in Morgan's the owner of the restaurant cannot manage the books, and is completely unaware of how much they lost in the past three years. This is simply bad business practice.

A friendship founded on business is a good deal better than a business founded on friendship.

John D. Rockefeller

Mixing business and friendship is not only dangerous in the restaurant business, but applies to all ventures, irrespective of their kind. Rockefeller's quote illustrates that business should come first. To put it in the words of billionaire investor and entrepreneur Carl Icahn, "If you want a friend, get a dog." However, there are also many examples of successful companies where the co-founders were close friends. For example, Apple's founders, Steve Jobs and Steve Wozniak became friends during a summer job, while Microsoft's co-founders Bill Gates and Paul Allen were close childhood friends. Furthermore, HP's co-founders Bill Hewlett and Dave Packard became close friends during a two week camping trip just after graduating from Stanford's engineering program, before they started HP, and Ben Cohen and Jerry Greenfield, co-founders of Ben and Jerry's Ice Cream, were inseparable childhood friends, who even double dated. The question that arises after this apparent paradox, how did they make it work? According to Shontell (2011), friends-in-business should recognize their individual limitations and respect what the other brings to the partnership. Anne Field (2010) identifies four pitfalls that are aligned with the principles that we have identified under X-factor 7: Teamwork, and are as follows: (1) not pinpointing roles, (2) failing to discuss long-term goals, (3) not stipulating how to make decisions or resolve disputes, and (4) giving short shrift to your partnership agreement. From a more personal perspective, Burbach (2012) stresses the importance of (1) mutual respect, (2) establishing boundaries, and (3) establishing friends only time. In our opinion, the most important aspect in mixing business and friendship is communication. That is, as long as there is open and honest communication, both about the business and the friendship, it can and most likely will work. However, this does not mean that it is easy to keep an open channel of communication, especially when pressure mounts and stress increases.

II. PRELIMINARIES TO CHANGE

Now, we will leave the illusionary world of ideal restaurants and turn to the actual subject of this book, organizational turnarounds. We will closely follow the stages of organizational change as defined by our dynamic control model of turnaround management (see Figure 7). For every stage we will discuss the most important techniques Gordon Ramsay uses to reach the stage's objectives. However, before we start discussing the various changes of organizational turnaround, we need to discuss two overarching principles that are applicable to all stages of change and which should never be forgotten. The first is, "All Change Comes from Within," and the second is labeled, "All Change Triggers Resistance."

Change Principle 1: All Change Comes From Within

In The Mixing Bowl, a restaurant in Bellmore, NY, Billy is the owner and chef. On the second day of the turnaround, Gordon Ramsay gathers Billy and wife Lisa together and shows them a map of the area that he (and his team) has put together. The map shows that when The Mixing Bowl opened, ten years ago, there were only four restaurants in the downtown area. Nowadays there are 41 restaurants in the same area. This vividly shows that the level of competition has dramatically risen. To cope with this increased competition The Mixing Bowl has to find its own niche. Gordon, "You have to reposition yourselves. What do you see in your neighborhood? …. Spa's, and gyms. What don't you see in your neighborhood? You have to do something with health. Give the neighborhood what they want." Then Gordon Ramsay starts a creative competition with Billy. They both create a healthy dish and, after tasting both dishes, Gordon suggests that both dishes are good enough to go on the menu. This example shows how Gordon tries to ensure that his suggestion is internalized (i.e. made his own). First, he makes sure that all the evidence is there for Billy to reach his own conclusions. Second, he emphasizes the fact that this is what the neighborhood wants/needs, not something that Gordon wants. Third, he immediately starts cooking with Billy. Hence Billy can become better at cooking healthy dishes and start to enjoy this, thereby making the value proposition of a healthy restaurant his own, not something which was forced on him by an outsider.

One of the most difficult tasks of a turnaround or change manager is to create sustainable change. Enabling sustainable change is an art form and requires deep knowledge on what to say or do at what moment. The change manager should possess a rare mixture of intelligence, diplomacy, and entrepreneurship. The problem with imposed change is that it rarely works. Providing ready-made solutions frequently fails for a number of reasons. First, ownership for the change rests with the wrong party. If you are going to behave differently, then it needs to come from you, rather than based on someone else's reasoning. Second, when change is imposed, change will most likely be resisted due to the not-invented-here (NIH) syndrome (Wastyn & Hussinger, 2011). Third, imposed change inhibits learning. If a solution is provided to us every time we have a problem, we will never learn to think for ourselves. In order to create sustainable change, the challenge is to let the other party arrive at their own solution. To do this, the turnaround manager first has to understand what is going on in the mind of the other party. The problem is that this way of coaching is often time consuming, while time is typically scarce in a turnaround situation, as bankruptcy needs to be avoided. In many of the episodes you see Gordon and the other reality TV turnaround managers struggling with this balance between imposed changes and changes from within.

A Zen Buddhist opened up a hot-dog stand and his first customer paid with a £20 note. After waiting, the customer demanded, "Where's my change?"
"Sir," replied the Buddhist, "all change must come from within."

The Wizards Handbook of Oracle Creation

Making sure that the owner of the restaurant takes ownership of the turnaround process is not easy. There is a strong tendency for the turnaround manager to take over the role of the owner and demonstrate leadership, especially when the owner is not performing (a root cause of the problem). Taking over responsibility is a very hazardous move, because such a temporary seizure of power will allow the owner to persist in denying the problems exist. The turnaround manager then has to impose all the changes. Although the restaurant initially seems to be performing better, in reality the restaurant is worse off. The owner and staff have not changed their ways and, more importantly, the cause and motivation for durable change (i.e., financial distress, dissatisfied customers) has disappeared due to the efforts of the turnaround manager. Under no circumstance should the turnaround manager take over the role of the owner, because the owner has to manage the restaurant when the turnaround manager has left. The responsibilities of the turnaround manager are clear-cut. The turnaround manager is a temporary figure employed to diagnose the problems, prescribes the cure, supports the organization, and coaches the key individuals. But the turnaround manager should not/cannot do the work of owner and staff. This is the golden rule of turnaround management. At the same time this is perhaps the most difficult rule to uphold. Even experienced turnaround managers, including all our TV-stars, sometimes make the mistake of taking over the role of the owner in order to speed up the change process and show owner and staff how a business ought to be managed.

It is critical that before a turnaround manager starts operating, a psychological "contract" is agreed between the owner and turnaround manager. In this contract two components should be clearly described. First, the contract should state the preliminary framing of the problem. The frame of reference in the beginning of the turnaround enables you, as manager, to see as possible remedies. Therefore, it is important that this frame is not too narrow. The frame of a turnaround should explicitly include the possibility that the owner may be part of the problem. In fact, in the majority of turnarounds the most important task of the turnaround manager is to change the behaviour of the owner. Second, the contract should state clear expectations regarding the role and added value of both the owner and the turnaround manager. Although, the turnaround manager will provide objective advice to the owner, the owner will need to take full responsibility for decisions made, he or she needs to understand that changing a business requires hard work, commitment, and, above all, the willingness to change as a person. It should be clear that the turnaround will not be an easy ride. The turnaround manager is there to help and support the business with expertise, but the turnaround manager should not and cannot take over the role of the owner. It should also be very clear that the turnaround manager will walk away from the business should the owner not want to help him- or herself and does not listen to the advice of the turnaround manager.

An interesting example illustrating the importance of the contract arrangement, can be found in the episode on Hot Potato Café. This restaurant in a suburb of Philadelphia,

Pennsylvania (USA) is owned by three sisters (Claire, Erin, and Kathryn) with no previous experience who believe the restaurant provides a relaxed retreat for the local community. That was eight months ago. Alas, they quickly discovered that having a restaurant requires serving good food. A couple of weeks after the opening the local paper wrote a terrible review. Since then, there have been few customers at Hot Potato Café and the sisters don't know what to do. They sunk their entire lives' savings, over 100,000 dollars, into this restaurant and now there is nothing left. To get the restaurant back on track, these ladies have brought in Gordon Ramsay. "Having Gordon Ramsay here is like winning the lottery for us," said one of the sisters. Gordon starts by asking the ladies what the problems are with the restaurant. The only thing he gets back is total silence. No one seems to be willing to give the real reasons why the business is failing. Gordon says that when he starts a turnaround usually the owners have some idea what the problem is. He's shocked that they don't even have a clue. There seems to be no passion left in any of the sisters nor is there much family love left in this family business. One of the sisters explains, "We do not like our company anymore." Gordon knows that he cannot help them unless they are willing to pull their weight. So, he tries to get some sense of commitment and willingness to work hard, and explains to them, "I need you to fight ... I cannot work with corpses, have you given up?" He continues, "This is not my restaurant ... this is your restaurant." As he receives no answers he decides to walk out of the Hot Potato Café and stop the turnaround effort right there and then. As he gets a few blocks down, the sisters run after him, determined to get his help and their restaurant back. Gordon explains to them that, currently, in his view, there is no passion or heart involved in running the restaurant, and explains very clearly, "I cannot give you that." The three sisters start crying and admit that they have lost the passion. But they say that they are tired and frustrated. This does not mean that they do not care for each other or the restaurant. Gordon puts this in plain words: "I cannot help any of you, if you cannot help yourself….are you committed? I am 100% committed to all three of you. In return I expect 200% commitment of you." Only when they fully agree, does he decide to go forward.

This episode of Kitchen Nightmares shows the importance of the contract and enforcement of it. By walking away, the three sisters are confronted with the fact that they actually may go bankrupt and that the family bond may end in tears. The solution they have hoped for, Gordon Ramsay, just walks away. This breaks them. They realize that they cannot turn the place into a profitable restaurant without Gordon Ramsay. They need to adapt. For Gordon Ramsay, walking away is an important test of the sisters' willingness to save the restaurant. By forcing them to speak out, the three girls start to understand that they have to be fully committed to their business, they need to take control as a family team, and that they have to stop pampering each other. If Gordon had not walked away, the turnaround would fail with Gordon Ramsay as the only person pulling his weight.

Gordon walking away is more than a trick. As a turnaround manager you always have to be willing to withdraw from a turnaround if you feel that the owners (management) are not committed to the change. You can feel sorry for them, but you cannot take up the baton and seize full responsibility. In Kitchen Nightmares there are various episodes where Gordon threatens to leave a restaurant, endangering the turnaround. This threat usually helps. In such circumstances, an owner becomes aware of the limitedness of his or her options, and makes it painstakingly clear that if Gordon walks away, bankruptcy and hardship are just around the corner. Although most owners (managers) do not really want to change, at that precise moment they realize that the consequences of not changing are even worse.

Gordon: *Scott, I am not your voice, I am not here to blow smoke up your ass, this is your responsibility. You bought into this. You have taken this on your shoulders.*

Scott: *Absolutely, I have had this conversation a couple of weeks ago to clean this kitchen and get it ready for service.*

Gordon: *Scott, you have to get real! Scott, you have got to get real! I am so f**king annoyed. This is disgusting.*

From: The Priory

Owner and former actor Allan Love has invested over 140,000 pounds in Ruby Tate, a restaurant that loses over 1,500 pound a week. Allan has borrowed another 30,000 pounds, but when that is gone, it is game over. To save the business, Gordon revamps the interior, but Alan does not like the new decor and simply says that it should go. After a hefty argument in which Alan acts like a baby, Gordon defies Alan, "Kick me out of the f**king door. At times like these, I feel you deserve to sink," and walks out of the restaurant. Later that evening Gordon tries to reconcile with Alan by taking him to a very successful fish restaurant. Gordon again explains that he is not there to get personal with Alan, but that he is there to help him. During the conversation Gordon's proposed changes to décor and menu are finally accepted by Alan. This creates room for Gordon to continue with the turnaround.

The above examples show that the turnaround manager must always be willing to stop the endeavor if the necessary conditions for change are not met. If the owner is not prepared to change or fully committed, the turnaround manager should stop working as this is a breach of contract. But, in practice, it is often the case that the turnaround manager is not willing to abandon the turnaround as the manager may be financially dependent on the job. Nevertheless, continuing with a turnaround without the owner's commitment and willingness to change is bound to fail.

In daily business life there are many examples of turnaround managers that have shown willingness to walk away from the task at hand. Steve Jobs called himself interim CEO (iCEO) for almost two years when he returned to Apple. This title constantly reminded the board of directors of the fact that he could walk out of the turnaround at any point in time. Moreover Steve Jobs effectively threatened the board on several occasions to follow his suggestions and made clear that he was prepared to step away from the change efforts. "My way or the highway" is sometimes a great slogan adopted by successful turnaround managers.

Change Principle 2: All Change Triggers Resistance

La Lanterna is an Italian restaurant that is heading toward for bankruptcy, as it is being run by two immature little boys that do not seem to have a clue what it actually takes to run a successful business. Head-chef/owner Alex is so worried about his business that he has not slept well for four months. For the business to run smoothly, the restaurant has to be well-managed by the maître-d. But, maître-d Gavin is Alex's best mate, it is his first job as a restaurant manager, and he does not have a clue. Worried about his utter incompetence, Gordon decides to give Gavin some coaching. His first words are, "You jumped up little prick. Who the f**k do you think you are, because you, as a maître-d, are f**king useless." Gavin smiles quietly, as he does not know how to respond. Gordon adds, "I have done it to upset you, so that you can come back to me." After these harsh words, Gordon invests a couple of hours training

Gavin to express himself, so that he can start earning the much needed respect and authority of his staff, and customers.

Organizational change always implies individual change, as it requires a change in the behaviour of the individual within the context of the organization (otherwise, the change would not be truly organizational). Psychology teaches us that behaviour is tied to an individual's beliefs and values, entailing a connection between an individual's behaviour and his or her beliefs about him or herself (i.e., his or her self-concept or self-image) and the world (i.e., his or her world view) and his or her emotions (as the behaviour fulfills or violates his or her values). Radical behavioural changes thus imply radical changes in one's concept of self, the world, and the emotions that one experiences. For most individuals, this is not a comfortable situation and it creates a great deal of uncertainty, fear, and frustration. A natural reaction is to resist these changes, to protect your self-image and model of the world, and prevent strong negative emotions. Resistance to change is a natural response that indicates that insufficient attention is paid to coach the individual to make the required transformation. Individuals need to be informed, educated, trained, and coached to effectively deal with the required changes. In the words of Sun Tzu (1971), "Supreme excellence consists in breaking the enemy's resistance without fighting."

It is important to note that organizational change will not only trigger changes within the individual for which it is intended, but change will also affect the individual's social environment. After all, an individual does not exist in a social vacuum, but is embedded through his or her ties with colleagues, friends, and family. Therefore, it is important to consider whether the individual can effectively deal with the resistance that s/he might face in his or her social environment.

There is not always a rational link between the size of the change and the magnitude of the resistance it invokes. Organizational change is especially able to trigger fierce resistance if the implemented change impacts an attribute or aspect of the organization where the individual has made a significant emotional investment. This emotional investment is a result of a process of identification, which can be defined as the unconscious modeling of thoughts, feelings, and actions to attributes of the organization (i.e., the restaurant) that leads to an emotional association (Merriam-Webster, 2012). There are different kinds of associations, some relate to the periphery of our being (example) while other relate to the core of our being. For example, if an individual's self-image and self-worth is attached to the organizational attribute, then the emotional attachment is likely to be much greater than when an individual identifies his or her peripheral individual features to organizational attributes.

Significant resistance to change is more likely when owners and management have experienced success in the past. More often than not, owners (managers) tend to equate the past success of the organization to their individual characteristics, and use it to enhance their feelings of self-worth. If success eventually turns into failure, this failure threatens the inflated self-image and self-worth because they have crafted their self-image on the success of the organization through the process of identification. To protect the positive self-image and the positive emotions, they deny the failure (i.e., reality) to feel comfortable, safe, and certain.

The path of least resistance is the path of the loser.

H.G. Wells

A case that demonstrates that all change creates resistance can be found in the case between famous football star Johan Cruijff and the Board of Commissioners of the club in 2011. After an impressive football career with Ajax Amsterdam and FC Barcelona, Johan Cruijff became a great football manager, first at Ajax Amsterdam (1985-1988) and then at FC Barcelona (1988-1996). At both clubs he was very successful with novel, attractive styles of play. After his active career as a manager he remained a powerful figure behind the scenes at FC Barcelona and played a very active role in making this club the greatest and most appealing club in the world.

But in 2010 his old love and football club Ajax Amsterdam lost 5-0 to Real Madrid. This triggered Johan Cruijff to offer his help in bringing his childhood club back to the European top. Considered by many to be the savior of the club upon his return, he was quickly appointed as a member of the board responsible for all technical matters by the general member council of the club. However, within months of his start, a conflict arose with the newly appointed Board of Commissioners about choosing a new general manager. Johan Cruijff argued that Ajax Amsterdam is at the core a football club and that business success or failure can ultimately only be found in the clubs ability to win games. Johan Cruijff argued that, as the person responsible for all technical matters in the board, he should at least have a voice in the appointment of the general manager. But the other four members of the board (responsible for marketing, legal, and operational issues) did not agree. They saw it is their responsibility to govern the club and select the general manager. They argued that Johan Cruijff, although seen by all fans as the potential savior of the club, was merely responsible for matters purely technical. They made the case that the general manager has nothing to do with football matters and therefore they wanted to appoint someone else. At this point Johan Cruijff decided to ask the general member council of the club for a vote. Either you want me to turn this place around, or you put the other members of the board in charge, but you cannot have both. Johan Cruijff understood that in order to change something fundamentally you need the full commitment of everybody in the organization. If commitment is not there, you need to stop the effort there and then. Obviously the members fully supported their savior thereby firmly establishing Johan Cruijff's power and ability to turn the club around.

III. DIAGNOSIS

After the contract is signed, and the turnaround manager wants to start the assignment, the first thing a turnaround manager has to do is to assess the situation. Where are the biggest problems and how severe are they? There is a whole set of practical techniques that a turnaround manager can use to spot problems. To continue with our medical analogy, let us have a look at the diagnosis of a patient by a doctor. The doctor always asks the patient (if possible, of course) what is wrong, to understand the symptoms of the disease. However, a doctor cannot diagnose a patient merely by a description of the problem by the patient. Instead, the doctor conducts a number of tests to determine what is actually wrong with the patient. To be able to determine what is wrong with a patient, the doctor needs to know the anatomy of the human body, and more specifically, the anatomy of a healthy human body. The same principle applies to organizations, which is why we have described the anatomy of a healthy restaurant in the previous chapter. Diagnosing a restaurant thus implies comparing the anatomy of a healthy (i.e., successful) restaurant (i.e., its ideal state) with the anatomy of the failing restaurant (i.e., its current state).

Although a doctor holds the anatomy of a healthy human body in mind when diagnosing a patient, and he realizes that an ideal or perfect state of health can (almost) never be achieved. The reason is twofold. On the one hand, it might be that a disease can never be fully cured. For example, viruses can never be cured because they reproduce inside cells, and action cannot be taken unless you want your body cells to be damaged or destroyed.[1] On the other hand, not many people are willing or even able to put in the effort required to achieve such a state (e.g., to do the required physical exercise and only eat healthy food). Hence, in diagnosing a patient, a doctor always forms another image, based on what is attainable by this particular individual. Again, the same principle applies to organizations. While it is helpful to have an ideal and perfect state of the organization or restaurant in mind, one should always realize that this perfect state can also never be attained, because there are limits to what (an individual within) an organization can achieve. This is dependent upon the resources and capabilities that are available in the internal and external environment of the organization (i.e., which resources and capabilities can the organization realistically access; e.g., make, buy, or ally). Therefore, when diagnosing a failing restaurant or organization, one needs to determine the desired (i.e., attainable) state of the restaurant. That is, the state of the restaurant where it is considered to be healthy (enough).

---

[1] In contrast, bacteria can be cured and killed, because they don't reproduce within cells.

Much like a doctor asks the patient to describe the symptoms of the disease, when a change or turnaround manager diagnoses an organization, s/he also wants to hear from management and staff what (they think) is wrong with the organization, to become aware of the symptoms of the failing organization. Again, it is impossible to determine what is precisely wrong merely on the basis of their verbal descriptions, for a number of reasons. First of all, if they would actually know what is wrong, why is there still a problem? That is, you simply cannot expect that they know what is precisely wrong and what needs to be changed. After all, they are not experts, and the mess that they are in proves this beyond doubt. The second reason is that you cannot trust anything they say, because, as explained in the introduction, people can be in denial and distort reality to accommodate their beliefs and values and to minimize any discomfort. Hence, the description that they give of the situation is probably not an accurate reflection of reality. Initially, because you cannot tell who is telling the truth and who is not, a turnaround manager should not trust anything owners, managers, and staff say. Clearly, you do want to register what they say, as this provides you with information as to who has a firm grasp on reality (i.e., after you have discovered what reality looks like for yourself). While it might be possible for them to determine why the restaurant is failing at this moment, this is no guarantee that they actually hold the recipe for a successful restaurant. After all, knowing what to change to avoid failure is not the same as preparing the restaurant for success in the long run, and beyond initial success (i.e., quick wins). To illustrate, when success increases and the restaurant becomes busier, stress is placed on the restaurant and its staff, and procedures and routines need to be in place to effectively deal with this pressure. If staff has not learned how to effectively deal with this stress, they tend to quickly revert back to their old patterns of behaviour.

In the diagnosis stage of a turnaround, the role of the turnaround manager reflects the skills of a doctor attempting to make a diagnosis or a detective trying to discover the chain of events that led to the crime. To find out the root cause of failure within an organization, much can be learned from applying the 'ABC' of detective work:

A detective's ABC: A) Assume nothing, B) Belief no-one, and C) Check everything.

Detective superintendent at Durham Constabulary (UK)

Regarding (A), we suggest following Sherlock Holmes primary intellectual detection method of abductive reasoning. Abduction is a form of logical inference that goes from data description of something to a hypothesis that accounts for the reliable data and seeks to explain relevant evidence (Doyle, 1986). In abductive reasoning, unlike in deductive reasoning, the premises do not guarantee the conclusion. Abductive reasoning can be understood as inference to the best explanation, such as the principles of economy and simplicity. In other words, through abductive reasoning, the simplest and most economical explanation is found that uncovers the chain of events. Of course, this does mean that more emphasis is placed on the need to check, i.e., (C), as mistakes can be.

In this chapter, we outline a number of principles that can be used to diagnose problems within a restaurant. We do this without total reliance on the viewpoints of others, in order for you to decipher the information and form your own opinion as to what is wrong with the restaurant. Using this as a platform, you can then compare your own diagnosis with that of others we describe, thus enabling you to determine the description that best reflects reality. This provides valuable information, as this lets you know whose opinion or help can be used later on in the change process. It is important to note that a diagnosis of the current state of the restaurant is not only used to understand the major problems the restaurant faces, although this is the primary goal. A secondary goal of diagnosis is to prepare the organization, its management, and its staff for the organizational changes that are about to come. As discussed, change often triggers resistance as an individual's mind-set (i.e., his beliefs, values, identity, self-image, and world view) is challenged. Often, this is accompanied by a strong emotional responses (i.e., stress) as people resist being pushed out of their comfort zone. Too much resistance might undermine the whole process and result in mutiny by the restaurant's owner, management, and staff. This resistance should be dealt with as soon as possible.

If Gordon is extremely critical and foul mouthed when inspecting the hygiene in the kitchen, this is not because he is upset with the sloppy standards, but also because this provides Gordon with an opportunity to see whether owners and staff are willing to accept his mind-set or frame of reference (i.e., that Gordon is the expert) and to gauge any resistance that might surface from a clash of mind-sets (or a mismatch in frames of reference). Hence, during the diagnosis stage, besides evaluating the state of the restaurant, Gordon is looking for ammunition to blatantly attack anyone who will trigger resistance to the changes he will implement at a later stage.

As the famous saying goes, there is no second chance to create a first impression. This is the phase of the turnaround were you have to execute several things correctly. Being a turnaround manager in this phase is the equivalent of a high ranked chess player in a simultaneous chess game. While you are diagnosing the seriousness of one problem, you are in the process of identifying new ones, and trying to get people out of their comfort zone by confronting them with your diagnoses. In addition, at the same time you are implementing you first set of improvements, you still need to prove your credibility as a turnaround manager. This is a frantic, exciting, and confusing period in the transition towards a new organization.

Change Principle 3: Experience Being a Customer

La Riviera tries to introduce fine French dining in one of the smallest cities of Scotland (Inverness). Its kitchen is filled with the best French chefs, ingredients are flown in from France, and the food is fit for a king. Unfortunately, the restaurant is empty. While the owner and head chef are baffled by the empty seats, after one view of the menu, Gordon spots one of the problems. The menu is in French, a language that a typical Scot does not speak. Hence, the customers have no clue what to order. Gordon decides that it is time to turn the tables, and to prove his point, he gives the front-of-house a menu of classic Scottish dishes written in the local Scottish dialect, and asks the French front-of-house staff which dish hey would like to have. They don't have a clue. Gordon asks them whether they have any idea what he is trying to convey to them. They get the point. It is difficult to make a choice if you do not know what is on the menu. Gordon agrees, and adds, "It is difficult for f**king Scotland to understand you guys."

Many restaurants fail because they are completely unaware of the experience which they give customers when visiting their restaurant. Simply taking the time to place one-self in the shoes of potential customers would prevent many failures, as most of the problems of the restaurant will quickly become apparent. For this reason, Gordon Ramsay often instructs failing restaurateurs to enjoy an evening out in their own restaurant. The quality of a dining experience is determined by our sensory perceptions, and a good experience satisfies all of our senses. Not only the gustatory (i.e., taste) and olfactory (i.e., smell) inputs need to be of high quality. Attention also needs to be paid to the customer's visual, auditory, and kinesthetic sensations. After all, if one of our senses is not satisfied, our whole dining experience can be a disaster.

The principal reason for a disastrous dining experience is awful food, which, at the extreme, can even provide a serious threat to our health and even life. A striking example is provided in the episode on Fiesta Sunrise, a Mexican eatery in West Nyack, New York. "It's disgusting," Gordon concludes after finding enough precooked beans to feed an army that seem to have been in the fridge for over a couple of weeks. "I care for the restaurant," the head chef explains to Gordon. In response, Gordon challenges him to take the beans to the customers, to see how they feel about this situation. "That's embarrassing," the chef replies. "Then why are you serving this," Gordon asks and he takes the beans into the restaurant and tells the customers to stop eating. After seeing the beans, the customers are disgusted, and quickly put down their forks and spoons.

A cardinal rule of cooking is to taste all the food that leaves the kitchen, to make sure the food meets the quality standard and to be aware of the customer experience. If you do not taste of the food yourself, how can you improve the quality of the food and prevent repeating the same mistake. In many failing restaurants, the head chef does not taste the food that leaves or is returned to the kitchen, and is thus completely unaware of the customer experience.

Even if the food is excellent, a dining experience can become a total disaster due to the presence of foul odor. This is because our gustatory and olfactory senses are intricately linked to one another, bad smell prevents us from being able to enjoy a fine dish. In the 1960's, Seascape restaurant – the oldest in Islip, New York – was truly buzzing. On Saturday nights, customers were standing in line outside the restaurant, in hope of being able to experience the vibrant atmosphere and taste its quality food. Things have changed a lot since then, and, unfortunately, not for the better. Many factors contributed to the failure of this restaurant.. The owner is timid, the head chef is incompetent, and the sous-chef couldn't care less. To make matters worse, a sewage smell penetrates every corner of the restaurant. "There is a really bad smell," Gordon explains to the waitress. "Sewage," she replies, and adds, "I cannot even believe customers come in here."

While our visual, auditory, and kinesthetic senses are not directly linked to our sensation of taste, they do color our experience as they provide the background or context in which our experience takes place. Annoying sounds (e.g., the irritating buzzer in the Sandgate hotel, the noisy desert display case in La Frite, and the loud music in the The Runaway Girl), visual disasters (e.g., the fly swarm in Dillons, the psychedelic wall-paper in The Dovecote Bistro, and the ghastly purple restaurant called Moore Place), and kinesthetic horrors (e.g., the touchy and sweaty waiter in The Olde Stone Mill) also inhibit a fine dining experience.

The Importance of Context

Context is highly important in determining our experience. For example, consider the following figure.

$$
\begin{array}{c}
\textbf{12} \\
\textbf{A } \textbf{13 } \textbf{C} \\
\textbf{14}
\end{array}
$$

The central character in this figure can be read as the letter B or the number 13, depending on whether you read across or down. Your experience of a situation (the B/13, in this case) depends on the context within which you interpret that situation.

Often, staff is unaware of the important aspects that can actually make or break a dining experience, because they are too busy getting the job done, and correcting urgent matters that go wrong in the failing restaurant. Therefore, it is important to experience being a customer yourself. Only then can you become aware of these things because you are in a different state of mind. That is, you have a different frame of reference with (or context from) which you interpret the situation.

Customers perceive service in their own unique, idiosyncratic, emotional, irrational, end-of-the-day, and totally human terms. Perception is all there is!

Tom Peters

Another useful instrument to diagnose the state of a restaurant (or business) is to visit a successful competitor. This creates a benchmark and enables a comparison of the failing restaurant with a successful one, and much can be learned in becoming aware of the differences between both restaurants. For instance, amongst others, the quality of the food, the freshness of the ingredients, customer service, ambiance and atmosphere, interior design, and the speed of the kitchen. All these characteristics can be easily observed when visiting the successful restaurant as a customer. Obviously, much more can be learned when the restaurant can be visited as a colleague, such as, for example, the workings of the kitchen, the coordination between front of house and the kitchen, the role of the expeditor in controlling the flow in the kitchen, the preparation of certain dishes, the preparation for dinner service, the storage of products and ingredients, the order management systems, et cetera. The possibilities are endless. For example, in La Lanterna, Gordon takes the owner and head chef Alex to a successful Italian restaurant to demonstrate the full meaning of quality Italian food, effectively installing an achievable objective or goal in Alex's mind to work towards his own restaurant.

While the most obvious strategy is visiting a successful competitor, it is also possible to visit any successful business, from a different industry. This strategy is more appropriate for improving an established business, because the similarities are less obvious, and one needs to translate the success from one setting to another, which requires creativity and imagination. It is precisely this creativity and imagination that is important in the process of innovation to increase the success of any business.

Change Principle 4: Ask Your Customers

Sabiatello's is a small little Italian restaurant that is located in Stamford, Connecticut. Unfortunately, things are not really going as planned. About as much food is coming back into as going out of the kitchen. One of the plates coming back into the kitchen is a lamb dish that is cold in the middle. Sammy, the owner of the restaurant, instructs his chef to put the dish in the microwave for ninety seconds. He does as instructed and the plate is promptly returned to the customer. The customer is a bit surprised because the plate came back so quickly. She touches the plate and feels that it is warm, which makes her suspect that the plate has just been put in the microwave, instead of putting the lamb chops back into a pan. She decides that she does not want it anymore, and the plate comes back into the kitchen for a second time. Now, it is Sammy's turn to be surprised. "First it is too cold, and now to warm, or what?" Sammy asks the waiter. The waiter tells Sammy that she doesn't want it, which really gets Sammy going. "Now it is too much cooked or what? How did she want it cooked in the first place?" he asks the waiter. The waiter remains silent, and Sammy decides to ask the customer himself. "How did you want your meat cooked?" Sammy asks the customer. "Medium rare," she replies and after Sammy asks her if she want another dish, she responds, "I do, but I don't want you to stick it back in the microwave." Sammy replies, "No, we are just going to make you a new one. Nobody is talking about microwaves. You are the one who is talking about microwaves." She responds, "They came out of a microwave, otherwise they wouldn't be exuding heat." Sammy replies, "Do you work for a microwave company? You know so much about microwaves." After a couple of seconds, Sammy looks the customer in the eye and says, "Unbelievable, unbelievable," and he walks away. The surrounding customers cannot believe what just happened, and start talking to one another about Sammy's rudeness. When Sammy comes back into the kitchen, he is still furious and instructs his chefs: "Let her wait."

Although we all know the phrase "the customer is king," in most organizations this mantra is not appreciated fully. For example, in Kitchen Nightmares, the majority of restaurateurs simply disqualify customer complaints, and classify them as absurd and/or false (e.g., in the case of Sammy, still under the impression that the food was okay, he actually classified the customer complaint as trying to get a free meal). Another example is Abby from Down City, who is so convinced that the food is perfect that she classifies Gordon's complaint about the food as, "Blah blah blah," and simply moves on with her business.

Obviously, when asking for feedback, it is important to take it seriously, and not to instantly dismiss it as either absurd or false, like in the examples above. Much can be gained from taking your customers' opinions seriously. First, getting to know what they really think of the restaurant provides valuable information about what can be improved to increase customer satisfaction. The success of any restaurant ultimately depends on its number of customers and how much they spend. Thus, being able to get direct feedback from your consumers to increase their satisfaction provides restaurants with a golden opportunity to increase revenues right then and there. Such an opportunity should not be wasted, and many entrepreneurs – especially the ones where production and consumption do not take place in real time in the same building – are extremely jealous of such opportunities.

Second, taking customer complaints seriously can prevent you from becoming delusional in the first place, and to keep a strong grip on reality. For example, at PJ's Steakhouse, despite the fact that on a regular basis many customers complain about the food and return dishes, head chef Eric still proclaims that his "food is wonderful and that people come from all over just to eat his cooking." One of the reasons that such a belief can survive is by distancing yourself from any complaints. Distancing yourself can be done both physically, like in the case of Eric, who does not interact with customers directly, or mentally, like Abby, who classifies all complaints as either jealously or absurdness. To actually keep a firm grip on reality, instead of distancing yourself, you need to listen seriously to any complaints that might arise. Instead of interpreting complaints from your own frame of reference, take some time to understand the customer's frame of reference instead, by placing yourself in their shoes.

The third reason to take customer feedback seriously is that this is also provides for an opportunity to find out what kind of food that they want, and how much they are willing to pay for it. For example, in La Riviera, the chefs are living in a dream, by thinking that local Scots are willing to pay top prices for the pretentious French food they are offering. To burst their bubble, Gordon decides to head for the streets, and ask locals about the food and what they are willing to pay for it. How far should you go in terms of taking customer complaints seriously? After all, like Sammy suspects, some people try to get a free meal. Consider the following example from Kitchen Nightmares.

Campania is an Italian restaurant in Fair Lawn, New Jersey. During dinner service after a successful turnaround, all customers are really enjoying their meals, and compliments fill the air, except for one table. At this table, everyone is complaining about the food, and plates are returned to the kitchen. The restaurant staff cannot believe what is happening, and decide to ask Gordon for advice, and shows him one of the plates that was returned. Gordon inspects the food, and sees nothing wrong with it, and confronts the customer. "The food was terrible. It was the worst food I have ever eaten," the customer explains to Gordon. In an effort to defuse the situation, Gordon suggests the woman to sit down and enjoy a coffee. When she still complaints, Gordon responds, "Madam, unfortunately, you are talking out of your rear," and adds, "You are just looking for trouble." New customers arrive and Gordon welcomes them, and adds "I am so sorry about the old bag."

All effective and engaging learning experiences provide frequent and meaningful feedback. Without feedback on whether or not one is getting closer to a goal, progress is unlikely.

Skype

This quote is taken literally by Skype, the Luxembourg-based Internet service company that provides free and paid VoIP (Voice over Internet Protocol), which allows customers to communicate over a network, like the internet. After each communication, Skype allows users to rate the communication in terms of quality, and provide feedback about the experience. Skype uses this feedback to continuously improve their products and services. With over half a billion customers, who all have their own opinion on improvements, Skype has to do extensive research to analyze the data and make sure that improvements work for the majority of customers. In addition, Skype also provides for a support network, which contains an online forum where users can post questions, comments, feedback, and complaints that are taken seriously and followed up by Skype staff. By listening seriously to customers, Skype is able to continuously improve service and increase subscribers each month.

Change Principle 5: Observe Up Close and Personal

Gordon is inspecting the walk-in fridge of The Secret Garden located in
Moorpark, New York. He doesn't really like what he sees, and asks owner and head
chef Michel, "When was the last time it had a really good sort-out?" Michel responds,
"Ehm, ehm …, yesterday." After discovering several mold-infections, Gordon explains
to Michel, "It is really important that you are honest to me. Every time I say something
to you all you do is smile to me. When are you going to get serious Michel?" "I am
serious," Michel answers. "No, you are not," Gordon replies, and while he shows
Michel another disgusting item in the fridge, he adds, "If you were serious, I would not
find this."

To get a handle on what is going on in the restaurant (or any business, for that matter),
it is important to observe up close and personal. The reason is that a failing restaurant
always implies that certain staff members (often the owner and management) do not

have a clue what is going on in the restaurant, either because they do not care or because they care too much and have gone into denial because reality is too confrontational. It is insufficient to ask management and staff about the problems, as their words cannot be trusted.[2] As the saying goes, "actions speak louder than words." For this reason, Gordon always inspects the fridge and kitchen for himself, and watches the staff perform during dinner service, to find out what is happening in the restaurant, who is doing what, and who or what is causing the main problem.

Because the kitchen is the heart of the restaurant, Gordon spends most of his time there to examine how the chef interacts with his staff, how he (or she) manages the process, controls quality, trains, instruct, motivates staff, and so on and so forth. Besides paying attention to how staff perform during service, Gordon inspects the ingredients in the freezer and storage room, checks the cleanliness of the oven, looks for dirt behind the stove, checks for labels on food in the freezer, et cetera. All these clues are hints as to the functioning of the restaurant and the people in it, and in this way, Gordon can get to the bottom of it all, and find out what needs to be fixed, who needs help, who doesn't, and to determine the priorities (i.e., where to start). Furthermore, it also provides the objective information (or 'ammo') that Gordon can use to confront people, gauge potential resistance, and facilitate change.

To continue with our previous example, after observing dinner service in the Secret Garden, Gordon asks Michel, "I observed tonight, communication was zero, there was no control. Do you think this is a f**king game?"

---

[2] It is important to get the opinion of management and staff about the problems in the restaurant, as this provides a rough guideline as to where to look for the problems. In addition, this information can provide a clue as to who actually has a firm grasp on reality, and can be trusted later on in the turnaround process.

At Sushi-Ko, while observing dinner service, Gordon notices that the wooden chop sticks have burn marks on them. Owner Akira explains that they save the chopsticks, wash them, and give them to new customers. Gordon is disgusted, and points to bits of food that are still stuck on some of the chopsticks, while explaining, "you never reuse some else's wooden chopsticks!"

At the Spanish Pavilion, Gordon tastes his first course of lobster bisque, and hates it. He actually suspects that it might have been dead before it was cooked, and asks the waiter about it. The waiter explains that the lobster came from the tank (aquarium), and thus was alive before they cooked it. Gordon decides to inspect the tank (aquarium) and asks, "Is he dead," while pointing to a lobster in the tank. "No, I think they are just sleeping," the maître-d responds. "Are you sure, he looks to be dead," Gordon asks again. "We keep a good eye on this," a nearby waitress interjects. "Surely not," Gordon responds as he picks out a dead lobster from the tank. Gordon explains that the other lobsters have probably been feeding of this dead one, and that the whole bunch might be infected.

Even one well-made observation will be enough in many cases, just as one well-constructed experiment often suffices for the establishment of a law.

Emile Durkheim

Observation is not only important in the restaurant business. Observation is an important trait of any successful entrepreneur. According to Stanford professor David

Kelly (2001), observation is the most overlooked phase in the product development process. He and his team also observe customers in their natural environment, instead of inviting them into a sterile lab for product testing. Observation is also a key to innovation, as many new products have their genesis in simple observation (Kadavy, 2011). This is exemplified by the numerous innovations that stem from an observation of our natural environment, and utilizing the processes we find there for economic and commercial purposes. For example, researchers from university of Akron have generated various innovations by simply observing spider weave webs (Blackledge, 2012). IDEO, the award-winning global design firm which helps organizations innovate says the following: *"We are not funs of focus groups. We don't much care for traditional market research either. We go to the source. Not the "experts" inside a company, but the actual people who use the product or something similar to what we're hoping to create. It's precisely this observation-fueled insight that makes innovation possible. Uncovering what comes naturally to people. And having the strengths to change the rules"* (Tom Kelley, 2001).

Change Principle 6: Put Pressure on the Organization

The Granary is a restaurant with 200 seats in Titchfield, England. Owner Nigel is a self-made entrepreneur who did run a successful business. Unfortunately, The Granary is not contributing to his success, and Gordon has the daunting task to fill its empty seats. On top nights, The Granary serves an average of 40 customers, which is not nearly enough to cover the costs to keep the place open. To get a feel for how the kitchen performs, Gordon decides to invite almost a hundred customers, and fill some of the empty seats. Head chef Martin told Gordon that he can cope with 200 customers, but collapses in the face of half of that number, and actually leaves the kitchen during service (hereby breaking a cardinal rule in the restaurant business, which is to never leave the kitchen during service). Nigel also does not want to take responsibility, and starts blaming Gordon for the disaster. "We have been stitched up. We have never had a night like this Gordon, I swear to God," Nigel explains and continues, "We never had a night like this. What were you thinking, ninety f**king people, without giving us any notice?" Gordon replies, "There are still fifty that haven't even been served, so why are you blaming me for this." Nigel doesn't cool down and still blames Gordon for the chaos in the kitchen. "You are a weak man. Why don't you open your eyes, get your head out of your arse, and try to look at your business objectively," Gordon says. Later on, Nigel explains "I know what he is doing, and I realize the reason for why he did it tonight. He needed to see what would happen when he would push past breaking point."

When diagnosing a patient, a doctor first asks the patient to describe the symptoms, after which the doctor examines the patient by measuring some of the more obvious vital signs, such as, for example, his or her heart beat and breathing. Next, the doctor checks other obvious signs that might indicate illness, such as, for example, swollen glands. If nothing is found, the doctor can conduct a stress test, where the patient has to perform a number of exercises (e.g., a treadmill test, a chemical stress test, or a cardiac stress test) to see how the body of the patient responds to stress. Hence, to determine what is wrong with a patient the doctor places the body under stress, as this will make certain malfunctions due to a disease more apparent.

In a similar vein, it is also possible to put pressure on an organization, to see how it performs under pressure. There are numerous ways to put pressure on individuals, staff, and the restaurant. For example, in D-place, Gordon has the kitchen perform a dry run test to cook the new specialty (a club sandwich) in a certain amount of time under pressure, while at Oscar's the head chef needs to cook lunch for 15 surprise guests (i.e., his family) so that Gordon can see how he handles himself under pressure. At La Parra de Burriana (Spain), Gordon invites the English expats from the Donkey

Sanctuary back, which is nerve racking for the owner and staff because of the incredible screw-up with them during a previous event. Stress-testing serves a number of purposes. First of all, as explained in chapter one, restaurants are characterized by periods of extreme pressure as customers expect high quality products and service that need to be delivered almost instantaneously. A good restaurant needs its staff to be able to perform under pressure. In the episode on the Glass House, Gordon Ramsay explains that a "good team delivers food under pressure." To test the performance and ability of a restaurant, you need to test all aspects of the business under stressful conditions.

Increasing pressure on a restaurant is the perfect means for Gordon to gauge where they stand in the turnaround process, and to identify the parts that need further work before operating smoothly and being able to handle the associated pressure. For example, in Clubway 41, by putting head chef Nigel under pressure, Gordon finds out that he already needs help with 20 customers, "let alone 250 to 300 customers a day." At a later stage, Gordon invites 50 influential people to see how far the restaurant has come in making the required changes. At La Riviera, Gordon invites influential business women to put pressure on the restaurant so that he can identify any cracks that are still present, and at The Priory, in line with the church décor, Gordon invites the Bishop of Sussex and Vickers to put some pressure on the restaurant and gauge their standing in the turnaround process.

Second, increasing pressure also teaches the staff that it requires hard and constant work to satisfy customers and makes staff more aware where they actually stand. This is absolutely necessary in a turnaround, as restaurant staff can get too euphoric as a result of the first successful, smaller changes, such as a new dish. They might start to develop unrealistic expectations about the restaurant and their capabilities. Stress testing helps to keep their feet on the ground, and show the staff that more effort is required to turn the restaurant around.

Third, if owners and staff make mistakes during high pressure events, Gordon is able to teach them a valuable lesson. This lesson is that a single mistake is not the end of the world, and they cannot afford to have one (minor) mistake determine (i.e., ruin) the rest of the service. In other words, he is able to show them that everybody makes mistakes – for example, consider the saying, "where wood is chopped, splinters must fall" – and life simply goes on. Gordon explains in the episode on D-place, "you can't let one misfortune let everything f**k-up." We all make mistakes and how we deal with them when they occur is what determines the difference between success and failure. For example, at Sushi-Ko in in Thousand Oaks (USA), Akira takes charge of the kitchen, and all seems to go well. Soon, however, Akira is overwhelmed, and his leadership starts to crumble, and with no leadership, the kitchen falls behind. Gordon steps in and has some words with Akira. This enables Akira to get his composure back, and to successfully complete the dinner service.

The better a man is, the more mistakes he will make, for the more new things he will try. I would never promote to a top-level job a man who was not making mistakes … otherwise he is sure to be mediocre.

Peter Ferdinand Drucker

Putting pressure on organizations and individuals is a common technique in environments where lives are at stake. For example, in the military, drill instructors often go to great lengths to increase the pressure on individual soldiers to gauge their behaviour in stressful situations. After all, life and death situations induce great deals of stress, which needs to be proactively appraised to prevent mental breakdown in real-life situations and guarantee the safety of others. Furthermore, specific exercises are developed to simulate real time situations as much as possible. Using pressure weak links and areas for improvement are identified. These methods are also used by the police and emergency services.

It is perhaps surprising that this effective principle is scarcely used in business domains. Sometimes application is somewhat difficult, especially if there is a time separation between production and consumption. For any business, the proof of the pudding is in its eating, i.e., the consumption of its products and services. Consumption provides the ultimate test of performance and enables identification of any weak spots that may exist in the production process. However, a creative interpretation of this principle allows a more universal application. For example, in an effort to assess a sales department, one could decide to place several 'fake' sales orders to gauge performance. Or one can 'invent' a campaign to see how the call center functions under stress. The only limitation is provided by our imagination.

Change Principle 7: Bring In Outside Expertise

Piccolo Teatro is a small vegetarian restaurant in downtown Paris, France. Owner Rachel is losing nearly 5,500 pounds each month, the debts are spiraling out of control, and the restaurant is heading towards bankruptcy. The disorganized kitchen is run by the owner's best friend Daniel, a Brazilian nutcase, who not only cooks bad food, but does so with a shocking attitude. To make matters worse, Rachel and Daniel fight constantly over the food in front of customers. "Welcome to the madhouse. [...] If my chefs, mr. Guy Savoy and mr. Joël Robuchon could see me right now, they would beat the crap out of me," Gordon informs the viewers.[3] Gordon is able to convince Rachel that Daniel needs to go, and she fires him during service. There is just one little

---

[3] Gordon was trained in Paris by Mr. Guy Savoy and Mr. Joël Robuchon. Guy Savoy is the Head Chef and owner of the eponymous Guy Savoy 3 Michelin star restaurant in Paris. Joël Robuchon operates a dozen restaurants in Hong Kong, Las Vegas, London, Macau, Monaco, New York City, Paris, Taipei, and Tokyo, with a total of 26 Michelin Guide stars among them – the most of any chef in the world.

problem, he does not want to leave. "Are you seriously kicking me out," he asks and starts to laugh. He then starts harassing the customers. Clearly, he has no intention of leaving. After some skirmish in the kitchen and restaurant, Gordon explains, "It looks like I am going to have to take Daniel to the nuthouse myself," and actually picks him up and carries him away over his shoulder. Daniel wants to come back in again, but Gordon manages to close the door just before he can enter the restaurant. Lacking a head chef, Gordon takes over in the kitchen. Fortunately, help is underway. Rachel's father Brian has found a new head chef, a 23 year old girl named India, who is eager to make the restaurant a success, and wants to learn French as soon as possible. With the help of India, the Piccolo Teatro relaunch is a big success, and Gordon's only worry is whether Rachel is really up the task. When Gordon returns six weeks later, there is bad news, the restaurant is closed. For India, there is some light at the end of the tunnel, as Gordon decides to hire her for his London restaurant.

Turning a failing restaurant into a successful restaurant is not an easy task. Even an experienced chef and entrepreneur, like Gordon, has to rely on the help of an outside team of experts and professional occasionally. There is no shame in asking for help, and to rely on outside experts when needed. In many cases, failure could have been prevented if restaurant owners would have acted much sooner. Basically, there are two reasons to bring in outside expertise, namely (1) to diagnose the problem, and (2) to fix the problem.

Diagnose the problem
Just like someone who is sick will go to a doctor to diagnose the disease or illness, a failing organization can get an expert opinion to diagnose the causes of

underperformance. This is the reason why the restaurateurs in our episodes have asked for help. The use of expertise in turning the restaurant around from start to finish is thus the most obvious example that can be taken from our reality TV shows. Because our turnaround managers (and the teams that they are using) have so much experience with running a business, the use of additional outside help, besides the turnaround manager, does not always become obvious. However, there are some exceptions. For example, in the episodes on La Riviera and Trobiano's, Gordon uses a food critic to get an objective, expert opinion on the quality of the food, while in Oscar's he uses the head chef's family to get a critical and honest voice about the quality of his cooking. Furthermore, at La Gondola, Gordon brings in Joe Barnes (who does all PR related activities for Gordon's restaurants) to help with the restaurants PR and to identify its key communication and marketing strengths (i.e., the fact that the restaurant is family run and has a dance floor).

Fix the problem
If the restaurant is missing some of the basic capabilities you would expect of a restaurant, outside expertise becomes a necessity. In this case, there are basically two alternatives. First, to replace the employees that are not functioning properly. For example, the replacement of India with Daniel at Piccolo Teatro was needed to have any chance of success. Another example is PJ's Steakhouse, where the restaurant is in dire need of a new head chef, as the old one is completely incompetent and the quality of the food is the main reason why the restaurant is failing. Second, staff can be trained so that they acquire the capabilities to put the restaurant back on track. For example, at the Priory, Gordon takes the kitchen staff to an expert who teaches them about the

meat on a cow. At The Sandgate Hotel, Gordon brings in his talented maître-d, Jean-Baptiste, to help with the service in the dining room.

If you need to take a step back from day-to-day operations and plot out the long-term direction of your user experience strategy, consultants can give you a perspective you cannot get on your own.

Jesse James Garrett

The use of outside expertise is common in all industries. Consider, for example, the wealth of consultancy bureaus. Precisely which consultant to hire is an extremely important, but difficult choice. What is needed most is someone who is able to get to the cause of the problem, instead of treating its symptoms. Many consultants or 'so-called' experts merely identify quick wins that can be easily achieved by placing a band aid on the sour spot, without providing a solution to the underlying cause of the problem, and often make it worse. As the proverb goes, "desperate times call for desperate measures." There are also many consultants whose strategy it is to listen attentively to the solution that management likes best, and then accommodate their analysis to this predefined solution. Clearly, this is not what is needed. What is actually needed is someone who is honest, righteous, and direct. This can be very confrontational, as he or she might conclude that you (i.e., the owner or management) are actually part of the problem.

Change Principle 8: Get to the Bottom

La Lanterna is a little Italian restaurant in the wealthy town of Letchworth, England. From an early age, head chef and owner Alex dreamt of being a chef, and during his childhood holidays, he fell in love with Italy. So much so, that he even started to call himself Alessandro. "I do think I am a pretty decent chef. I know what works and what doesn't, and I take a lot of pride in what I do," Alex proclaims at the beginning of this episode of Kitchen Nightmares. His style of cooking is Italian, so Gordon immediately asks the obvious question, "And you are from, Italy?" Alex responds that he is from England, and explains, "I have always worked in an Italian kitchen, and so I have learned the language and learned the style of cooking." "So lots of Italian ingredients," Gordon wonders. "Yes," Alex answers confidently. Curious about the origin of the ingredients, Gordon inquires as to where they are from, only to find out that they are from Tesco's, a large UK based supermarket chain. "Lemons from Sardinia?" Gordon continues to ask. Alex answers that the lemons are bought at the Cash and Carry (i.e., Makro). Not very pleased with this answer, Gordon explains to Alex, "So far, I have seen f**k all Italian." Alex swallows in silence. Later on during the episode, after being seriously disappointed by the food he tasted and being confronted with the hygiene nightmare in the kitchen, Gordon says to Alex, "You say you want to run it as the Italian restaurant, but it is nowhere near it." In his defense, Alex replies, "I was taught by a very well respected Italian chef." "That's total bullshit, because there is nothing Italian here," Gordon concludes, "Nothing anywhere." To get some more perspective on the situation, Gordon decides to look for this well respected Italian master-chef. Gordon discovers that this so-called master-chef is Italian born cab-driver Mario, for whom cooking was not more than a temporary profession to make some extra money. Gordon comments; "Alex needs to bite the bullet, and relaunch the restaurant with a fresh identity ... of his own."

Before changing anything, it is important to know what is actually going on, and to define the root cause of failure of the restaurant. This is not an easy task. A failing restaurant (or business) always implies that management is in state of denial, and that they do not have a firm grasp on the actual cause that is leading to failure. If they did, they would simply tackle the issue and the restaurant would not be failing in the first place. Hence, words cannot be trusted, you need to dig deeper by double checking everything that has been said and get to the bottom of it all. "Spare the rod and spoil the child" is perhaps the most apt saying. Desperate times call for desperate measures, and quick fixes only make matters worse. In the case of La Lanterna, Gordon realized that one of the root causes of failure was that Alex was holding on to the illusion that he was trained by a well-respected Italian chef, who taught him all there is to know about Italian cooking. This firm belief prevented Alex from having an open mind to

Gordon's expert opinion, to be humble in terms of his own capabilities as an Italian chef, and to be eager to learn about Italian cooking. To bring Alex back to reality, Gordon knew the only option was to shatter Alex's illusion, by exposing Alex's role model for who he really is, an Italian born who has utterly failed as a chef and is currently driving a cab.

At La Lanterna, Alex holds a (positive) belief about himself and his training which prevents him to see (i.e., deny) the negative aspects about himself and his cooking. The opposite can also happen, where we hold a negative belief about ourselves or a situation that prevents us to see any positive aspects. For example, in La Parra de Burriana, extremely bad food at a high price completely ruined a fund-raising Valentine's dinner for the Donkey Sanctuary, a local British expat club. Owner Laurence does not want to be reminded of this event. In his eyes, the relationship is completely ruined and can never be fixed. Obviously, he is in denial, and wants to distance himself from it as much as possible, because it reminds him of his own failure. However, a loyal local community is important for the survival of any restaurant, so Gordon decides to get to the bottom of it and find out the details for himself, and to see whether this relationship can be restored. Gordon is able to convince them to give the restaurant one more try, and invites them for the relaunch. The evening turns out to be a great success, and as one of the expats explains nicely, "If he can come up with this sort of deal, yes we will be back again."

One could argue that both Alex (La Lanterna) and Laurence (La Parra de Burriana) still were pretty young at that time, and that they did not have enough experience to prevent such a distorted view of reality. However, consider Abby from Down City, who has been in the restaurant business for 33 years. She is in complete denial and Gordon refers to her as "insane." If 33 years of experience in the restaurant business do not prevent an utter distortion of reality (e.g., she judges the quality of the food as 10 out of 10), what level of experience do you need? This implies that nothing can be taken for granted. A turnaround manager has to get to the bottom of the issue to uncover the real problem. Only this way can a turnaround manager determine who is telling the truth and who has a distorted view of reality (and may require some serious therapy).

As discussed, all successful change comes from within (see change principle 1), and the restaurant's owner and staff need to make it happen. A reality-check can be found in the episode on Morgan's, a restaurant in Liverpool, England. The restaurant is being run by three women, but nobody knows who is in charge of running it, which is one of the main causes of the restaurant's failure. After watching a dinner service with many disappointed customers, Gordon asks Helen (one of the owners) how she feels about the situation. "It is diabolical. The whole thing is just a sham," she answers honestly. Gordon responds, "You are the most f**king honest person in here, you know that. And the more honest you are going to be, the more chance this place has got for f**king survival." It comes as no surprise that later during the turnaround, Gordon wants Helen to run the restaurant, despite the fact that her sister happens to be trained as a restaurant manager.

Another good example can be found in the episode on Rococo. Here, in response to Gordon's complaint about the frozen seafood, head chef Nick explains to Gordon that it is genuinely impossible to get fresh shrimps in King's Lynn, England and that he tried to find them. Gordon does not believe him and decides to go to the harbor himself (located only a couple of hundred meters from the restaurant) where he easily finds fresh shrimps. He buys the shrimps from a local captain and confronts chef Nick with the fresh food. The confrontation with his lies then opens possibilities to implement further changes for Gordon.

Another example can be found in the episode on The Fish and Anchor. Here, Gordon revisits the restaurant after six weeks, after a successful but heated turnaround with a tempered fighting couple. The couple explains that all is still going strong and that they haven't been fighting in the restaurant anymore since Gordon left. Instead of trusting them, Gordon calls the customers to actually find out whether they are telling the truth. In this case all customers reported good food, great atmosphere and no fighting.

Trust is good, control is better.

Ascribed to Vladimir Ilyich Lenin

From the sporting world there are many examples of the use of intense diagnoses to find problems and come up with creative solutions. Perhaps the most well-known, and most studied, example is the one of Billy Beane and the Oakland A's, a Major League Baseball team based in Oakland, California. Billy Beane has become famous as the General Manager of the Oakland A's. In 2011 even a movie (Moneyball) was made on about his analytical methods to craft a great baseball team. The legend of Billy Beane started in 1998 when he started adopting rigorous data analytics and mining techniques to predict the value of players within the context of a team instead of trusting the traditional ways of determining players' potential. Billy Beane's approach made the Oakland A's into a frequent title contender despite their small budget. His revolutionary approach transformed the game and many other general managers have followed his lead.

In the business world perhaps the best example of this principle ("Getting to the Bottom") is probably found in the application of the Six Sigma process improvement methodology. Six Sigma was originally developed by Motorola in 1986 and has now widespread acceptance in a range of industries. It's breakthrough came in 1995 when Jack Welch made Six Sigma the standard methodology of process improvement within General Electric. The Six Sigma methodology seeks to improve the quality of processes by identifying errors and removing its causes. A distinctive element of Six Sigma is that it uses rigorous data collection and statistical methods to get to the root cause of failures. This method has shown to lead to significant improvements in manufacturing companies, but Six Sigma is not very effective in service companies and in dynamic environments where the rate of technological change is high. But through its elaborate techniques it is often very effective in finding the evidence that supports the rationale for organizational change.

Change Principle 9: Get Into the Mind of People

Back at the Secret Garden, Gordon is seriously disappointed after tasting the food and decides to confront owner and head-chef Michel, "You seem proud of that food?" Michel explains that he likes it and thinks it is good. "Don't take this personally. I thought your food was crap. Tasteless, bizarre, your food was long winded, boring, and just badly done," Gordon responds. Michel is flabbergasted, and looks at Gordon like he wants to kill him then and there. Looking to resolve the tension between them waitress Jane interrupts, "As a waitress, I don't get complaints about the food. The only complaint I might get is that the food is cold." "Jane, I am not asking you to blow smoke up his asshole, I have just sat there for the last hour, and I have had one of the worst meals I have ever eaten." Gordon retorts. "That's a matter of opinion," Michel lashes back at Gordon. "If you are such a passionate chef, and you are a natural because you are French, and you love cooking, why are you serving tinned crab meat," Gordon asks. Michel explains that because the restaurant is quiet, fresh crab meat goes rotten quickly and he decided to buy the tinned variety instead. Gordon looks Michel in the eye and explains, "I am trying to get inside your mind, so I can start breaking down … how stupid you are." Gordon then adds: "We have got a lot of work to do in a very short period of time. All I need is, not some sort of French arrogance, I just need your support, and more importantly, your honesty."

To effectively change an individual, it is important to know what goes on in the mind of that individual. If you want an individual to change, it is not sufficient to simply explain to the individual what he or she needs to do. People do whatever they think is right, on the basis of the awareness that they have in the moment. To change their behaviour, we need to change their awareness, so that the change in behaviour makes sense to them, and they can see the added value that this will bring. After all, "you can lead a horse to water, but you cannot make it drink." Hence, there is a need to elicit their mental programs (and the beliefs and values that they hold) to understand the logic behind their behaviour. On the basis of this information, it becomes possible to tweak the logic of their mental programming, so that change becomes natural and automatic.

A nice example of how this works in practice is provided by the episode on La Parra de Burriana (Spain), where Gordon Ramsay quickly realizes that Lawrence's pride is preventing him to accept Gordon's ideas and suggestions. Gordon explains, "It's your pride that you have got to stop f**king worrying about. Cause how f**king proud are you going to feel, at f**king Malaga airport, with your bags. Then what are you going to do?" As the turnaround runs to an end, Gordon realizes that he has only one chance to get through to Laurence, to get his attention. Gordon takes Laurence to a bull ring, where Laurence has to fight a raging bull. Gordon explains to the viewer, "He wouldn't go into a bull ring without clear instructions from someone, who knows what they are talking about." After the events, Gordon inquires how Laurence feels, and the first thing he says is, "I feel your point has been proven." In this example, after realizing that it was Laurence pride that was resisting the changes, Gordon was able to 'attack' his pride head on. Gordon did so by providing Laurence with an experience where he actually had to swallow his pride to survive.

An additional advantage of getting to know what makes people tick (by eliciting their mental programs, beliefs, and values) is that we do not take their resistance personal any more. In French, there is a saying which goes "comprendre tout c'est tout pardoner," which translates as "to understand all is to forgive all." When we know the true cause of someone's behaviour (e.g., resistance), we no longer project our own insecurities onto the situation any more. It is for this reason that Gordon Ramsay often has family members write letters to other family members to let the other know what they think, belief, and feel. This way, the other person understands the cause of certain behaviour, i.e., why they behave the way they do. For example, in Giuseppi's, Gordon asks the father, mother, and son to write letters to each other, to explain their feelings and emotions, and has them read the letters to one another. This scene clearly demonstrates the release of tension that this brings, and how it changes the perception of one another. Another nice example is provided in the episode on the Black Pearl, where Gordon invites the owners and staff to write questions to any member of the restaurant on a piece of paper (anonymously). Subsequently, Gordon asks the addressed person in question. In this particular example, owner David refuses to answer one of the questions, after which Gordon confronts him and says that he is "full of shit." This way, thoughts and feelings are elicited (made explicit) from people's minds and the reasons and causes of behaviour become apparent.

There are different ways to get into people's minds. On the one hand, there is the direct approach, by asking questions about how they think, belief, or feel about a certain matter. On many occasions in Kitchen Nightmares, or the other reality TV-shows that we have watched, we do see the turnaround manager acting as some kind of therapist or coach, by eliciting someone's mental programs, beliefs, and values. On the other hand, there are also several indirect approaches. The approach that holds the most entertainment value is the provocative approach (see change principle #14). This is where Gordon Ramsay in particular lashes out at people, both professionally and personally, to get to know the real or true being (i.e., his or her beliefs, feelings, and emotions) that is hiding behind the mask that they have created for themselves. While Gordon Ramsay uses this abusive manner in any episode, the example above from The Secret Garden portrays this approach rather well. A second method is asking family, friends, and co-workers what makes someone tick and to behave the way that they do. For example, in PJ's Steakhouse, Madalyn explains to Gordon that Joe has given up after his brother PJ died. Madalyn explains that PJ owned a bar, and when it came up for a lease a few years after PJ passed away, they decided to rent the place and name it after PJ. This brought Joe back from being the walking zombie that he had become after they lost PJ. Gordon then uses this information and dedicates a corner of the restaurant as a tribute to PJ, which brings Joe back to reality and motivates him.

The first step to change is awareness. The second step is acceptance.

Nathaniel Brandon

Seeing the above, it cannot be a huge surprise that great leaders tend to ask questions rather than offering new solutions (Marquardt, 2005). By asking questions implicit assumptions are challenged and clarity about the subject is created. Moreover the ownership of possible solutions is shared with the staff. A great article in The New York Times describes the leadership style of IBM's former CEO, Sam Palmisano, and brilliantly demonstrates the power of asking questions.[4] According to Sam Palmisano four basic questions which he presented to the company's top 300 managers at a meeting in early 2003 changed IBM's culture and business strategy. These four questions were:

- Why would someone spend their money with you – what is so unique about you?
- Why would somebody work for you?
- Why would society allow you to operate in their defined geography?
- Why would somebody invest their money with you?

This simple set of four questions pushed management out of their comfort zone and focused their thinking. Leadership is more about asking the right questions than giving the right answers. The same is true about turnaround management; it is about asking the right questions, then the proper answers will reveal themselves.

---

[4] Even a Giant Can Learn To Run. *New York Times* (January 1, 2012).

Change Principle 10: Understand the Business

We are back at La Riviera, Inverness, Scotland. Basically, The restaurant functions as the playground of multi-millionaire Barry Larson, who made a fortune in fast-food restaurants, and has a long-lasting desire to own a Michelin star restaurant. To get these valuable stars, Barry has hired an ambitious young French chef, Loic Lefebvre, who had previously been a sous-chef in a three-star restaurant. Loic heads up a perfectly-trained and experienced all-French staff. However, the locals are not biting and the restaurant is losing over 8,000 pounds per week. The food is overpriced, is too complex, and has no direction. Loic has become uncontrollable and is desperate to impress. Gordon decides to confront millionaire-owner Barry with this problem and says him bluntly, "Start acting like a boss, not as a sugar daddy." Barry responds, "I am not in a position to criticize him." Gordon retorts, "But I am."

Another case in point is restaurant Lido di Manhattan Beach, in California. Owner Lisa is a business school graduate who took over the restaurant five years ago when she was 23 years of age. She has no prior experience in the restaurant business. In the five years Lisa has owned the restaurant she has made almost no changes. The restaurant still has the same name, décor, menu, and staff. After five years Lisa does not even understand the basics of the restaurant business. Gordon quickly discovers that there are some serious hygiene problems in the kitchen, and that the chefs are serving three day old tuna. When Gordon shows Lisa some of the disgusting things that are going on in her kitchen, she responds, "I did not know of all this going on, unless someone tells me so, but no one told me." Clearly, the relation between the two chefs, Luis and Arturo, and Lisa is not an open and honest one. Luckily, Lisa understands that she needs to improve and wants to learn how the kitchen works. It does not take long before she discovers that her chefs are not using fresh ingredients, and are heavily addicted to the microwave. The chefs have taken advantage of Lisa since she took over the restaurant, because she was ignorant as to the functioning of a vital part of her business.

The two examples above show how important it is to understand the business you are in. If you do not know what is going on, how can you make improvement? How can you challenge the status quo? How do you know what and whom to believe if your staff invents credible yet untrue stories? How can you bring your staff further? How do you know what works and how do you build a profitable business? A deep understanding of the business is especially important when you need to change. Chances are that senior members of your staff will deny the facts and resist any change. They will fabricate plausible, but false stories in order to escape change, and remain in the comfortable niche they have carved out for themselves. You need to be able to separate fact from fiction if you want to enforce a successful turnaround.

The only source of knowledge is experience.

Albert Einstein

It is not only to understand the business if you are running a restaurant, as this principle – like many others – also applies to other industries. This is confirmed by the work of Frederick Zimmerman (1991), in his study of successful business turnarounds. His study consists of 16 actual cases of distressed companies in trouble for at least 20 years. Nine of those made it and six did not. In his words, "Regarding the unsuccessful cases, there is evidence that management often did not know what needed to be done and did not know how to do what was needed. [...] In none of the unsuccessful cases did management display sufficient expertise in organizing the firm's production or in managing the firm's major business."

The major recommendation of Frederick Zimmerman for companies pursuing an organizational change is to find managers who really understand the business. He argues, "Don't assume that being smart is a qualifying asset in the long term. Successful management during a turnaround is partly a matter of domain. Key people should understand the business and the company's individual business in particular. The most successful turnaround agents were those who had experience in the industry being served."

IV. UNFREEZE

"Do we have a deal, Mr. Reagan," agent Smith asks Cypher in the movie The Matrix, when Cypher is about to betray Morpheus and Neo. "You know, I know this steak doesn't exist. I know that when I put it in my mouth, the Matrix is telling my brain that it is juicy and delicious. After nine years, you know what I realize?" Cypher rhetorically asks Mr. Smith. He then takes a bite of his steak, and, after a sigh of pure pleasure, adds "Ignorance is bliss." Agent Smith concludes, "Then we have a deal," upon which Cypher responds, "I don't want to remember nothing. Nothing, you understand."

The saying "Ignorance is bliss" means that not knowing something is often more comfortable than knowing it, and is the major reason why people go into denial. This process works as follows. When there is a dissonance between our beliefs (or knowledge) and the perceivable facts (i.e., when the facts conflict with our core beliefs), we become anxious, as these fact threaten what we belief (about ourselves and the world). To prevent this anxiety or discomfort, our beliefs are not to be doubted or questioned, and it is the facts that have to be altered (Nathaniel Brandon, 2001). For most, however, this decision is not as conscious as Cypher's decision to betray Neo and Morpheus. Instead, our unconscious mind simply distorts reality (i.e., the facts) to accommodate it to our beliefs. While this process brings comfort and safety (by preventing anxiety), it is also the enemy of choice and change. Deciding that our beliefs are true and to deny anything that says otherwise is, therefore, a dangerous strategy. Great accomplishments do not just spring up on-their-own, and hope is not a strategy. Answers don't come without questions, and questions don't come without awareness. The first step in the journey of change is awareness (i.e., the opposite of denial and ignorance), which starts by becoming knowledgeable about the basic forms of denial. This brings the process of denial into our consciousness, so that it can be managed. The basic forms of denial are: (1) simple denial, where we distort reality so that the fact disappears, (2) minimization, where we admit the fact but deny its consequence or seriousness, and (3) projection, where we admit both the fact and its consequence, but deny responsibility for it. If ignorance and denial prevent change, for change to occur, ignorance and denial have to be eradicated as much as possible, requiring: (1) awareness, (2) acceptance, and (3) responsibility (Branden, 2001).

Awareness implies that we are aware of the situation that we are in, by respecting the facts that exist. This is the practice of living consciously, of being present to what we are doing while we are doing it (Branden, 2001). For example, if a customer, supervisor, employee, supplier, or colleague is talking to us, we are fully present to the encounter. It also implies seeking and being eagerly open to any kind of information, knowledge, or feedback that is relevant to our interests, values, goals, and projects, not only of our external world but also of our internal world. When asked to account for the extraordinary transformation he achieved at General Electric, Jack Welch spoke of "self-confidence, candor, and an unflinching willingness to face reality, even when it's painful."

Acceptance refers to accepting the situation and its consequences, or the willingness to experience the situation and its consequences in its entirety. This means that we do not evade, deny, or disown our thoughts and feelings that this situation elicits, and that we stay away from self-repudiation, by giving oneself permission to think one's thoughts, experience one's emotions, and look at one's actions without necessarily liking, endorsing or condoning them (Branden, 2001). This will lead to non-defensiveness, as we do not experience ourselves as being "on trial," and also creates a willingness to hear critical feedback or different ideas without becoming hostile and adversarial.

Responsibility implies realizing that we are the authors of our choices and actions, and that each one of us is responsible for our own lives and well-being and for the attainment of our goals; that if we need the cooperation of other people to achieve our goals, we must offer values in exchange; and that the question is not "Who's to blame?" but always "What needs to be done?" (Branden, 2001).

In medicine, this principle remains the same. Before a doctor is able to effectively 'treat' a patient, the patient first needs to agree with the doctor's diagnosis, and become aware of and accept the disease. The patient also needs to take the responsibility to do what is necessary to be cured (e.g., by undergoing surgery, taking medication, and/or altering their behaviour). To make sure that the patient accepts responsibility of the disease, the doctors confronts the patient with the hard facts. This is usually done by explaining what the consequences will be if the disease is not treated (e.g., a stroke, a heart attack, or death). By dramatizing the consequences, the likelihood that the patient takes full responsibility for the disease increases, and chooses to do what it takes to prevent the consequences from actually happening.

What is needed to successfully change a failing restaurant is that its staff becomes aware of, accept, and take responsibility for the mess that they are in. In other words, they need to accept the brutal facts and stop the culture of denial that is ruining the business. This is, however, not easily accomplished. For people that have been in denial for a long time, change is not easy. Most of the people Gordon encounters in Kitchen Nightmares actually do not want to change, but merely want the symptoms (i.e., empty seats, financial distress, et cetera) to disappear. This explains why merely talking about a successful future (i.e., visioning) is hardly ever enough to get people out of their comfort zone on a voluntary basis. Hence, people have to be jolted out of their comfort zone, and both the carrot and the stick are necessary. Besides visioning (i.e., the carrot), what is needed is to increase the level of discomfort in the current situation so that people realize that the current zone is not comfortable at all (i.e., the stick). If we know that people choose comfort over discomfort, raising the level of discomfort to such levels that it surpasses the discomfort associated with the proposed changes, change will become automatic, as people will simply opt for the most comfortable situation. This requires techniques that might appear quite harsh for the untrained eye. For this reason, people either love or hate Gordon Ramsay's approach to turnaround (change) management. In our opinion, the ones who do not see through his verbal abuses are disgusted by his lack of respect and personal attacks, while the ones that look somewhat closer actually find the tough love that is needed to jolt people out of their comfort zone.

A scholar who cherishes the love of comfort is not fit to be deemed a scholar.

Lao-Tzu

The utmost importance of overcoming denial can also be found in programs of organizations such as Alcoholics Anonymous (AA). At the AA overcoming the addiction has to start with Alcoholics admitting that they have an alcohol problem. Admitting the problem is their first mandatory step to stop drinking. Only by openly admitting that they personally have a huge problem, the alcoholic shows he or she is ready for overcoming the addiction. This applies to a general principle: Only when people are shaken out of their comfort zone, they are ready enough to take the next step.

Change Principle 11: The Carrot ... (create Hope for a Better Future)

D-place is a nice little restaurant in Chelmsford, England, or so it seems. The food is awful, the service is bad, the staff is fighting, the kitchen is breaking down, and leadership is completely absent. The restaurant is failing, miserably. During the turnaround, Gordon introduces a new menu, and decides to train the kitchen staff to cook the new dishes. There is a positive vibe in the kitchen, staff is smiling, and for the first time in ages, head chef Philippe and maître-d Dave are not shouting at one another, but communicating in a civilized manner. The facial expression of the staff has changed dramatically since the beginning of the episode, as the trainings has given the staff a glimpse of what the future might bring.

Getting people out of their comfort zone is a difficult task. One of the things that is needed to accomplish this task is to create hope for a better future, by constructing an image of the future where life is comfortable, rewarding, and pleasant; i.e. the restaurant is successful, there is a vibrant atmosphere, and customers and staff are happy. This is the future that the individual wants to move towards and something he or she might even become passionate about. There are several ways to install such an image in the individual's mind. A highly effective approach is to create a collective experience of success, just what Gordon Ramsay did in the example of D-place above, so that all those involved in the experience start using their own imagination to construct an image of what the future could potentially bring. In a way, this is like being able to have a small taste of what lies in store for you. Once you have tasted something you like, you automatically want more, and start to imagine how life would look like if you did. A less effective approach is merely talking about what the future can bring. For most people, talking alone does not create an experience of success, as this requires a great deal of trust and imagination. For example, we have seen that owner Alan from Ruby Tate's actively resisted almost all changes that Gordon wanted to implement. He even kicked Gordon out of his restaurant, after a head-on collision over the seemingly trivial issue of a painting. But, after the successful re-launch of his restaurant, Alan comments, "Everyone likes the name, everyone likes the décor, and I am ready to throw the towel in." He smiles and laughs, and adds "So, it's good, it's good. So, well then Gordon, if you are in there, anywhere. It's obviously working. He is right, I am wrong, and it doesn't really matter, as long as we are going to make a success. That's all we need." In the case of Ruby Tate, the change is only accepted after experiencing the success of it.

In all things it is better to hope than to despair.

Johann Wolfgang von Goethe

According to the research of Jim Collins, truly great companies are characterized by The Stockdale Paradox. These companies confront the brutal truth of the situation, yet at the same time, never give up hope. The Stockdale Paradox is named after Admiral Jim Stockdale, who survived more than seven years as a POW during the Vietnam War and went on to be Ross Perot's running mate in the 1992 U.S. presidential election. Stockdale was tortured more than twenty times by his captors, and never had much reason to believe he would survive the prison camp and someday get to see his wife again. Here is the paradox, Stockdale noted that optimism is important, but at the same time the most optimistic of his prison mates were always the ones who failed to make it out of there alive. "They were the ones who said, 'We're going to be out by Christmas.' And Christmas would come, and Christmas would go. Then they'd say, 'We're going to be out by Easter.' And Easter would come, and Easter would go. And then Thanksgiving, and then it would be Christmas again. And they died of a broken heart." The Stockdale paradox demonstrates that, although hope of a better future is what keeps you going in difficult times, there is a need to confront the brutal facts of reality, and that hope is not an effective strategy.

Change Principle 12: And the Stick … (Confront with Undeniable Facts)

Campania is a nice little restaurant in Fair Lawn, New Jersey. The restaurant has been very successful, until eighteen months ago, when Joe, the new owner, bought the restaurant. It has been in steady decline ever since. One of the reasons that the restaurant is in financial distress has to do with the enormous amounts of waste. Joe prepares enormous amounts of food that perish in the freezer. Moreover the portion sizes are very large. Almost every customer leaves the restaurant with a doggie bag. Gordon tries to confront Joe with this. He sits down and orders up two appetizers, two entrées, and a bowl of antipasto. Gordon then calls Joe over to show him just how much food that is. The food fills up the complete table, and Joe cannot but admit that it is quite a lot of food. Gordon points out that this is where he is losing a lot of money. Instead of being happy with this valuable advice Joe is not pleased. This means that Gordon has yet to find another way to break through Joe's protective shield.

The above example shows that it is not easy to get someone who is in denial out of his/her comfort zone. At first, Gordon tries to find severe and cold hard evidence such as hygiene problems in the kitchen which cannot be denied. Additionally Gordon tries to make the dire situation as tangible as possible, in this case by having all the different plates of a single menu on one table. But even if reality stares these owners in the face, they keep changing the subject to stay in their comfort zone.

Gordon Ramsay uses a number of ways that enable him to confront the owners and/or chefs with reality:

- Confront with the quality of food and ingredients (precooked, not fresh).
- Confront with hygiene problems (filth, mold);
- Confront directly with customer reactions (often bad);
- Confront with reservation books (empty);
- Confront with financial data (books, bank accounts);

Confronting owners with financial records and bank accounts is often the most intense type of confrontation. A good example of such a confrontation can be seen in the episode on Morgan's, the restaurant in Liverpool, where Gordon accompanies owner Sandy to her home to analyze the books together. The administration is a total mess, and only there and then Sandy realizes that she needs to shape up or ship out. Regularly, Gordon invites the wife or husband of the owner to discuss financial matters together. This is important as in many cases the partner of the owner is completely or largely in the dark about the true financial state of the restaurant. The Dovecote Bistro (in Devon, England), owner Mike has to tell his wife Mo about the dire position of their restaurant and the fact that he has loaned an extra 80,000 pounds of debt on the credit card. His wife is furious as she was not told about the credit card loan. She gives Mike the choice, improve the restaurant and follow Gordon's advice or end the marriage. Gordon uses hard financial data together with personal relations to shock people into reality. Inviting the dearest and nearest (or other important stakeholders) is an effective strategy to really confront someone with cold hard facts. Beloved ones are generally not completely blinded to deny the prospect of impending doom and poverty, and will do whatever it takes to make the owner aware of the situation that they are in (see change principle #15).

Gordon also confronts owners with their dismal customer performance. For instance in Le Bistro, a Florida based restaurant, Gordon provokes owner and chef Andy by stating that he just doesn't care about his customers. The reaction of Andy is spineless. He shrugs and says, "Yeah, well that's just your opinion." When Gordon intensifies his provocative comments, Andy downright denies all accusations and, at the end of the day, even accuses Gordon of lying. In order to get through to him, Gordon tries a new tactic. Gordon invites Andy into a galley to meet the customers from the previous night. One by one, they describe the way they felt after they ate at Andy's restaurant: bad food, terrible service, and long waits. Instead of accepting reality, Andy is getting infuriated. He simply tells the customer that they are wrong and that they don't know what they are talking about. He absolutely refused to listen to any personal reviews of his customers. Although this did not jolt Andy back into reality, his levels of discomfort increased, and, with it, his readiness for change.

Another well-known tactic that can be used to break through the denial and lethargy of managers and owners is to invite mystery shoppers. Many of the turnaround managers in reality-TV shows use this tactic at times. Worth mentioning here is Tabatha Coffey who regularly sends in mystery shoppers to get their hair done before the real TV-turnaround starts. Using hidden cameras, the public can observe the (lack of) care of hairdressers. An example can be found in Tabatha's episode on Ten Salon in Long Beach, California. By confronting the hairdressers with the feedback of the mystery shoppers and the footage of the cameras, the hairdressers recognize their disgraceful behaviour and substandard work. The objective evidence of the video shooting combined with the personal feedback of mystery shoppers is very strong and leaves limited room for further denial.

These examples show that it is not easy to deal with people who have been in denial for so long. There often is a reason for near bankruptcy, these owners have been denying the true situation and avoiding well-meant advice for long. Do not expect that sound advice is well accepted if a company is truly in distress. Even if the evidence is clear, most of the subjects of the show will still do anything to avoid a confrontation with reality. It takes constant confrontation supported by hard facts before denial can be broken down.

Refusal to believe until proof is given is a rational position; denial of all outside of our own limited experience is absurd.

Annie Besant, English Philosopher (1847-1933)

Perhaps the best example of the principle of confronting with undeniable facts outside the restaurant business can be found in New York City's Police Department. In 1993, under then- Commissioner William Bratton, the NYPD introduced weekly citywide and precinct-by-precinct computerized statistical reports on crime (a.k.a., COMPSTAT). These factual reports where discussed in weekly meetings in which police commanders were questioned about local increases in crime. All in all this transformation of the NYD, with COMPSTAT as an essential element, lead to a spectacular crime turnaround, with murder down 68 percent and overall felonies down 50 percent in the five years since 1993. As COMPSTAT has become globally publicized, more and more international police forces followed New York's lead in using crime data and meetings to identify potential problems and evaluate the effect of police responses. It should be noted that the success of COMPSTAT is based on more than data analyses. It was the combination of rigorous analyses and forced confrontation of hard facts in weekly meetings which proved to be instrumental in changing the organization. Bill Bratton personally ensured that hard facts could not be denied anymore.

Change Principle 13: Internalize the Burning Platform

We are once more back at the Secret Garden (Moorpark, California). Owner Michel is still in denial, and unwilling to face the cold hard facts about his failing restaurant. During an inspection of the kitchen, Gordon is trying to break down Michel's defenses, and confronts him with the dismal hygiene, and asks whether Michel is serious about running a restaurant. Instead of accepting the severe state of his kitchen, Michiel asks whether Gordon's restaurants are perfect. Ramsay replies, "No. But at least they are clean!" Again Michel tries to duck the issue by changing the subject. He replies and says that his restaurant at least makes decent money. Here he goes in the wrong as Gordon knows that Michel is over $320,000 in debt. Gordon asks him how much money he has actually made. Michel is shocked by this question. He wasn't expecting this and so he simply doesn't answer. He keeps denying the facts by remaining silent. Gordon tries to confront Michel with reality while Michel disagrees and continues to reject Gordon's advice. After two days Gordon decides to try another approach; he hopes to shock Michel into reality. On the morning of the third day Gordon puts a lot of very visible foreclosure signs all over the building. Gordon hopes that the all too visible signs disturb Michel in such a way that he finally realizes that bankruptcy is imminent. Unfortunately, Gordon's scheme does not go as planned as Michel is several hours late for work. Michel does not arrive until ten-thirty and becomes very angry when he sees the signs. "This is not funny, I am pissed," Michel says to Gordon. "Good, you have got every reason to be pissed. I am glad you are angry. Finally you have woken up," Gordon responds and then asks Michel to image how bad it would be for the restaurant to close. "I don't see anything constructive here," Michel explains and remains pissed. Later on, the message has finally sunken in for Michel, and he comments, "If the restaurant were to close down, I don't know what I would do. I would feel ashamed."

If a confrontation with hard objective data does not provide a big enough stick to jolt people out of their comfort zone and back to reality, sometimes you just need to get a bigger stick. Whatever the means, what is needed is the creation of a so-called burning platform. For those that do not know the origin of the term, the story goes as follows (Conner, 1993: 43):

> *At nine-thirty in the morning, there was a catastrophe on an oil-drilling platform in the North Sea – just off the coast of Scotland – that killed one hundred and sixty-six crew members. One of the crew members that managed to survive the disaster was superintendent Andy Mochan, because after being violently awakened by the explosion and alarms, he ran straight from his quarters to the platform edge, and jumped from a height of fifteen stories into an ice-cold ocean*

that was covered by burning oil and debris. He knew that because of the water's temperature, he could survive for merely twenty minutes before hypothermia would kill him. When an interviewer asked him how he was able to take such a leap of faith, he replied, "It was either jump or fry."

Andy was able to jump because it was a matter of life or death. Staying on the platform was simply not an alternative, as death would surely follow. A restaurant that is on the brink of bankruptcy finds itself in a similar situation. It needs to change to survive, despite how frightening and threatening this might actually be. More often than not, however, due to their denial, management and staff do not fully realize that they are standing on a burning platform. That's why it is important to make them aware of the fact that the platform is burning, and to explain the dangers that are involved with this situation. This is the reason why Gordon always asks restaurateurs about the level of debt the restaurant has, how much time they have left before the place goes belly up, and what else (e.g., house, respect, and confidence) they would lose if the place closed down for good.

On many occasions, staff is completely unaware of the dire straits the restaurant is in, as they are kept in the dark about the levels of debts the restaurant is facing. While most restaurateurs feel it is natural not to share the financial situation with the staff, this is a dangerous situation. After all, this means that the staff is unaware of the danger that they are in. They do not realize that the platform is burning, and, as such, do not see any reason to change. To prevent failure, change is needed. However, change brings discomfort to all involved, and when staff feels that there is no urgent need for the change, they will resist it. For this reason, it is imperative that staff is informed of the impending doom looming around the corner, and that their comfortable life at the restaurant could soon be over. For example, at Dillon's, Gordon has been battling with general manager Martin along every step of the way. After some much needed changes, Gordon is again on a collision course with Martin, when owner Mohammed finally steps in and takes Gordon's side. "Thank you, Mohammed, I have been waiting for that for the past week," Gordon says. Now, Gordon finally has received the authority to create a burning platform for the restaurant's staff, and explains, "Now, I want to see positivity from everybody, absolutely everybody. And if there is anyone who doesn't think he can pull on the rope like that, look for a new job."

Confront them with annihilation, and they will then survive; plunge them into a deadly situation, and they will then live. When people fall into danger, they are then able to strive for victory.

Sun Tzu

Creating a burning platform implies making the status quo so uncomfortable and/or costly, that change becomes the only logical alternative. Major change is always costly, but when the status quo is more expensive, a burning platform situation erupts, and major change is no longer a good idea, but has become an imperative. This not only applies to organizational and individual change, but also to societal change (e.g., a revolution). In this case, a crisis is needed that jolts people out of their comfort zone into some kind of action.

It is telling that even something as rational as fundamental science sometimes needs a proper crisis in order to renew itself. This process is described by Thomas Kuhn (1962) in his famous book "The Structure of Scientific Revolutions." According to Kuhn, a scientific revolution occurs when scientists encounter anomalies that cannot be explained by current theories and the universally accepted worldview in which it exists. This means that progress is not just a matter of continuous improvement. Sometimes, improvements in science require a state of crisis. During this crisis enough space is created that allows the application of novel and revolutionary ideas. When these new ideas are capable of successfully in explaining the inconsistencies between reality and the old worldview, a new worldview or paradigm is accepted. This is, however, not as easy as it might seem. Using a quote from Max Planck, Kuhn (1962: 150) himself argues that, "a new scientific truth does not triumph by convincing its opponents and making them see the light, but rather because its opponents eventually die, and a new generation grows up that is familiar with it." This observation from the world of science underlines the difficulty of changing human beliefs, especially when these ideas are deeply ingrained in our belief system and identity. Sometimes man cannot be changed, but have to be replaced as we will see later in the chapter on change.

In recent times, the memo from (former) Nokia CEO Stephen Elop created an example of the burning platform.[5] A better example was the speech of former Chrysler CEO Bob Eaton. On July 17, 1997, he walked into the auditorium at company headquarters in Auburn Hills, Michigan, and gave the speech of his life. Instead of celebrating four years of progress, he warned of trouble brewing on the horizon. His speech was based on the nonfiction bestseller "The Perfect Storm," a tale of three fishermen caught at the confluence of three potent storms off the Canadian coast. Bob Eaton told senior managers that three factors threatened to sink Chrysler in the coming

---

[5] http://blogs.wsj.com/tech-europe/2011/02/09/full-text-nokia-ceo-stephen-elops-burning-platform-memo/

decade. "I think," Eaton said, "there may be a perfect storm brewing around the industry today. I see a cold front, a nor'easter and a hurricane converging on us all at once."[6] The cold front was chronic overcapacity, the nor'easter was a retail revolution that empowered buyers, and the hurricane was a wave of environmental concerns that threatened the very existence of the internal combustion engine. "Read The Perfect Storm, and you will learn".

Both Elop and Eaton's messages where so clear and so frightened that they allowed both CEO's to pursue new strategic directions. However, the room to maneuver does not mean that these new strategies are better than the old ones. In the cases of Nokia and Chrysler, we know now that these new strategic directions where not always the best answers to the problems. The merger between Daimler and Chrysler has been a mammoth disaster for both companies and Nokia's shift of its smartphone strategy towards Microsoft's Windows Phone 7 has been a failure up to now. Tomi Ahonen even argues that Elop's memo and subsequent strategic change will lead to the fall of Nokia: "Nokia is doing the most rapid death in the shortest period of time ever, for a global market leader Fortune 500 sized company. Ever."[7]

---

[6] Sydney Finkelstein, *The DaimlerChrysler Merger*, Tuck School of Business at Darmouth, Business Case Study 1-0071, 2002.
[7] http://communities-dominate.blogs.com/brands/2012/07/the-sun-tzu-of-nokisoftian-microkia-mirror-mirror-on-the-wall-whose-the-baddest-of-them-all-waterloo.html

Change Principle 14: Be Provocative

We are back at Fiesta Sunrise, a Mexican restaurant in West Nyack, New York. Gordon is disappointed after tasting the food, and when inspecting the kitchen and ingredients, Gordon becomes furious, as he is confronted with a serious health hazards. "Oh my God, what's that?" Gordon asks as he picks up what looks like a lump of pure fat. "Ground beef," owner Vick explains. Gordon doesn't believe his ears, and shouts at Vick "Ground beef …, you idiot, it's fatter than you." Vick remains silent. Gordon continues, "Are you f**king stupid?" Still, utter silence. The verbal torrent continues, but Vick doesn't budge and remains silent. Eventually, Gordon decides to shut down the restaurant. Vick, however, looks like a statue and is still completely unmoved.

This example is just one of many which shows that Gordon Ramsay can be very provocative in the way he confronts individual behaviour. This is probably one of the biggest critiques of Mr. Ramsay. Many people say that he shouts and curses far too often. Of course, this behaviour partly reflects the personality and upbringing of Gordon Ramsay. Even so, there are good reasons for his provocative manners. The purpose of this behaviour is to break through the shield of denial and to push people out of their comfort zone. In Gordon's own words when he turns Morgan's around, "I have to be cruel to be kind."

Consider twenty-eight year old owner Alex of La Lanterna, the Italian restaurant in Letchworth, England which (tries to) offers modern Italian cuisine. Alex himself is the head chef and the restaurant is run by his best mate, maître-d Gavin, assisted by Alex's ex-air hostess 'girlfriend' Emily. When Gordon tastes the food and is critical about it, Gavin begins to laugh. Gordon angrily responds, "Do you think this is funny?" and Gavin's smile instantly disappears. After two days of verbal abuse, owner Alex finally starts to crack. Gordon's behaviour immediately changes. Gordon now argues that Alex is in a unique position to regenerate and rejuvenate the restaurant. But he does not only give this positive message of possibilities. At the same time he keeps provoking Alex to get him moving. For instance, when he finds some lemons in the kitchen, he says to Alex: "That is how big your bollocks should be, find them and start using them." To Gavin, the maître-d, he says, "You look like a lost boy ... you need to have authority." To both he says, "You are so close to cowboys, put the restaurant up for sale." At the same time he emphasizes the fact that these provocations are not personal. "You are f**king useless. I am saying this so you can get back at me."

The behaviour of Gordon is well grounded in provocative therapy (Farelly & Brandsma, 1981), a therapy where the psychologist seeks out resistances in the client and then approaches what the client seeks to avoid, using improvisation, emotional language, and a great deal of humour. Provocative therapy teaches one not to be afraid and dig deeper. Stories should not be accepted at face value and there is no border between business and private areas as organizational change is always personal. Provocative therapy teaches the psychologist to be open, frank, and fearless in his questions and remarks.

Gordon Ramsay is certainly the most provocative and abusive turnaround manager on TV. In Kitchen Nightmares, there are many examples of his aggressive language. The following list of quotes may give some idea of his insulting tongue: "Get your head out of the sand and smell the coffee" (D-place), "You are not even capable of running a f**king bath" (The Granary), "As chef to chef, let's be honest: you can't call yourself a chef if you serve that shit" (The Priory), "Stop using your customer as a hairdryer, blowing smoke up your ass" (The Runaway Girl) ,"I never ever, ever met someone I believe in as little as you" (Peter's), "It is one thing to live the dream, another to be living in a dream world" (The Olde Stone Mill), "You are a happy to be fake chef" (Sebastian's).

It is noteworthy that Gordon Ramsay commences his confrontational conduct as soon as he enters a restaurant. This is even before he tasted any food. In 'Mojito' he enters the restaurant with the following remark: "This is an interesting décor: a garage sale went wrong." In Rococo he says to a nosy waiter: "You are like a haemorrhoid in my asshole," and to another nosy waiter in The Mixing Bowl he states: "May I ask you not to stare at me, it makes me feel uncomfortable like a cockroach running on my back." And confrontational language is used when Gordon gives feedback on the food. For example in Lela's he comments on the food, "What was fine dining about what I got today? OK, let's put it this way. I thought it was like a pile of shit, I was embarrassed for you." Another good example of the provocative feedback Gordon uses can be found in the episode on Anna Vincenzo's, a nice little Italian restaurant in Boca Raton, a very rich community in Florida. After the meal, Ramsay gathers the staff to receive the feedback. He starts with the awful salmon salad. CeCe, owner and head chef, replies that everybody loves that. Ramsay replies; "Who is everybody? Your restaurant is empty." Gordon says that the snapper was horrible. CeCe is in denial, although she didn't even try it, and the waiter agreed that it was soggy. CeCe defends herself and asks whether Chef Ramsay gets defensive when someone criticizes his food. He responds, "I do not cook shit like that."

It is not always easy to take such criticism, even if it is true, perhaps even more so when it is true. Nick, the owner and cook of Rococo, says after Gordon's initial assessment, "He could have said something positive to put our morale up. I do feel choked." Alan Love, the owner of Ruby Tate, says after the feedback of Gordon, "The food is probably not right and maybe it is full of crap, but it is just that I put my whole life in this restaurant." The harshness of the critique can sometimes suffocate people and thus initially prevent cooperation. But this frank criticism is often needed to get through the denial phase and get people moving. In The Runaway Girl, the owner, Justin, responds to Gordon with: "There are a lot of things I have been doing right." To which Gordon reacts, "There you go again. 98% of what you do is wrong. You are only in love with the idea of doing things right." Gordon Ramsay's verbal abuse sometimes goes along with rude behaviour. In the case of 'Lido di Manhattan Beach' he actually throws up when the eggplant is raw and the tortellini tastes like rubber. A little later, when he discovers a severe hygiene problem in the kitchen, he orders owner Lisa to close the kitchen ASAP. When she is reluctant to do so, he simply invites all the guests in the restaurant to have a look in the filthy kitchen, driving Lisa crazy and making her cry in the toilet.

Although many people resent Gordon Ramsay's behaviour, there is merit in this aggressive and annoying stance. This harsh criticism, right from the start, sends an important message to the owner, chef and members of staff; you are dealing with a serious guy. This is the real deal, the change will not be pleasant and you cannot make up any stories. And there is a second important function of his provocative behaviour: to get a better understanding of the personalities involved in the restaurant, and to assess resistance and identify room for improvement. As Gordon himself says in Rococo, "When I poke him, I want to wake him up, I poke him for reaction."

You cannot make a revolution with silk gloves.

Joseph Stalin

Perhaps Gordon Ramsay's behaviour and language can best be compared with the tantrums of Steve Jobs. Just as Gordon Ramsay, Steve Jobs could be very charming and had an astonishing ability to attune with various people. But, like Gordon Ramsay, Steve Jobs did not only use charm and creativity, but applied rigorous critique, and sometimes even outright intimidation to get what he wanted. The stories about Jobs' boldness are numerous. He did not only scream at employees, but would insult high-ranking business people without hesitation if he thought it necessary. Steve Jobs used any method he thought was most appropriate in a situation. The role of the "bad boy" was not only used to disarm other people and giving Jobs a slight advantage but, it was also used to push people beyond their boundaries. It was used so people would deliver more than they could dream of. Apple's Head of Design, Jonathan Ive, is very clear about this in Steve Jobs' biography (Walter Isaacson, 2010). The stubbornness and confrontational nature of Steve Jobs led the team at Apple to create better products which, would not have otherwise been achieved.

Change Principle 15: Involve the Social Context

Nick, the owner of Rococo, is in denial. Whatever Gordon suggests, Nick does not want to change anything. Gordon: "Nick needs a real kick….I am going to talk to his wife." In order to understand Nick, to identify his motives, to discover his passion, and to figure where his resistance comes from, Gordon really needs to understand which forces drive him and which forces hold him back.

Moreover, by explicitly asking the backing of family members for the turnaround, Gordon creates not only a better understanding of the psychology of the owner, but he also creates an extra set of change levers by involving family members. A nice example of "family assistance" can be found in the episode on The Dovecote Bistro. In this episode Gordon informs Mo, the wife of owner Mick, that her husband has already borrowed over 80,000 pounds on his credit card. When told about this credit card debt she steps in. She tells Mick: "You have to come clean. Tell me honestly, we have to pull together. I am not ending my life for you. It is absolutely imperative that you are open and honest with me so we can fight the battle together." She warns Mick and says him that he has to adapt if he does not want to lose his wife and daughter. This threat gives Mick the stimulus to really start the turnaround.

That nearest and dearest do matter in organizational change can be seen in the episode on The Seascape Inn, Islip, New York. The owners are Peter and his mother Irene. Irene remembers the good old days when her husband ran the place in the 1960s. But the happy days are now over and the place is near bankruptcy. In an effort to help Peter and Irene, Gordon tries to turn the place around but finds fierce resistance from the cooks, Doug and Charles, who treat Peter like a little boy. After two days of trying to turn the restaurant around, Gordon finally steps in and says that he can't help Peter with the turnaround with the cooks in the kitchen. He needs Peter to walk into the kitchen and fire both chefs. Peter first hesitates but then, timidly, fires them. Mother Irene is very happy that her son finally acts like a man. The next day Gordon goes boxing with Peter. At first, Peter is not aggressive at all and hits Gordon rather meekly. But then all of a sudden Peter starts to hit Gordon very hard and aggressively. After all the aggression is released Peter begins to cry. He explains his timid behaviour from his past. As a boy he never could do anything good. His late father told him constantly that he failed in everything. This upbringing led him to be 'nice' to everyone. His timid behaviour was there to keep the peace. Although Gordon turns the restaurant around, a couple of weeks after Gordon departure Peter sells the restaurant. After all running a restaurant was never his personal aspiration. He only ran the restaurant because he could not cope with his mother and the legacy of his departed father.

It is crucial to understand that change is always personal. You cannot separate your business life from your personal life. To truly understand a person and the reason why they behave, you have to have a full system perspective of that person and all the forces that influence this behaviour. By separating someone's business life from their personal life means that you cannot begin to truly understand that person. You may fail to spot the important switches for change and you will misinterpret behaviour and overlook the true reasons for denial and resistance. In the restaurant business, this is perhaps very obvious as many restaurants are family run businesses where it is hard to separate personal from business life. But in large corporations, it is almost never the case that the turnaround manager truly invests in understanding the behaviour of senior management. Typically change managers fail to take a true system perspective. The old saying *"behind every successful man is a wise women"* still holds true. If you really want to create a successful turnaround it is very necessary to include the partner of the owner in the turnaround. In a world where the work-life balance is stressed as both women and men have different careers, it is crucial to understand the personal situation of key people in a turnaround situation.

They say you are not you except in terms of relation to other people. If there weren't any other people there wouldn't be any you because what you do which is what you are, only has meaning in relation to other people.

Robert Penn Warren

Involving the social context does not only allow you to shake people out of their comfort zone, it is also helps address lethargy. Especially, if the role of the spouse increases and they become an important business partner. This is particularly true in family run businesses and young start-ups. Sometimes this role is obvious (e.g. Bill and Hillary Clinton), but in many cases the important influence of the spouse on strategic business decisions is well hidden. By involving the spouse you enable the owner to share problems and discuss solutions. As the spouse is often the Chief Trust Officer of the company, getting their perspective is important. But it is not only the spouse. Many CEO's mention not only their wives as key advisors, but often they say that their best advice comes from their mother or father. As an example Richard Branson, founder and chairman Virgin Group, claims the best advice came from his mother; "never to look back in regret but to move on to the next thing."

Change Principle 16: Test and Reward Fair Value

Neill Farrow is the owner of The Glass House, a restaurant in Northwest England. Neill is deep in debt, to the extent that he does not dare to switch on his mobile phone. Within a day Gordon has discovered one of the major problems in this restaurant. "Day one. Analysis ready. I need to start with that cocky chef." This chef is Richard, 37 years of age, good pedigree and well paid (25,000 pounds a year). But the performance of Richard is surely lacking. He is silent in the kitchen, the hygiene of the kitchen is poor, and his cooking is under par ("pretentious crap, lazy, and clumsy cooking"). Even Richard himself openly admits this by questioning his own ability and passion in the kitchen. Having a nonperforming, expensive chef in the kitchen is a major problem. According to Gordon: "The best investment for a restaurant owner is the chef. He is a major asset in the kitchen, motivator, leader, and he brings customers back in." As in so many cases, Gordon Ramsay finds fierce resistance. Richard does not

want to change at all and keeps denying problems even if they stare him in the face..
Moreover, he is too lacklustre to try new ideas. At the same time, he remains arrogant
as he feels that he cannot be missed as the valuable head chef he thinks he is. Richards
lofty but false opinion of himself is sadly shared by timid owner, Neill who does not
have the bollocks to argue with his highly paid chef. To teach Richard and Neill a
lesson, Gordon tells them to have some time together to quietly discuss the future of
the restaurant. Gordon therefore offers to cook in the evening so Richard and Neill can
have dinner together while Gordon cooks. But in reality it isn't Gordon who does the
cooking. Gordon has asked the apprentices in the kitchen to cook. The apprentices will
swap roles every 30 minutes so everyone does a certain role for a period of time. The
food turns out to be wonderful and Richard and Neill really enjoy it (thinking that
Gordon made it). Only after desert, when Richard and Neill told Gordon they loved
the food, Gordon tells them who actually did the cooking. This tactic of Gordon had
three great effects. First, the junior staff really started to believe in themselves as the
food was great and they managed to prepare and cook the food without the chef.
Second, Richard realizes that he is not as valuable as he thought he was; he can be easily
missed. The restaurant seems to be a happier place, producing better food without the
head chef. Richard now understands that he has to step up his performance to be really
worth the 25,000 pounds a year. Third, owner Neill realizes that he really does not need
Richard if the chef does not improve his performance.

Gordon tried the same trick in The Walnut Tree Inn in Wales. Here, owner Francisco
has lost his head chef, but he does not feel that one of the sous-chefs is capable of
becoming a head chef. As it isn't easy to find a great chef in Wales, Francisco steps in
and starts cooking himself under false pretenses ("Internally…I can only be the one').

This is clearly a bad idea as Francisco is a great maître-d, but a lousy chef. Gordon uses the same trick as in The Glass House. Again Gordon says that he will do the cooking for Francisco, but in reality the two sous-chefs Stefano and Gary will be doing the cooking. And again the food turned out great and the self-esteem of both sous-chefs increased tremendously. Alas in this case, although Francisco publicly admitted the food was great, Francisco still refused to listen to Gordon and give both boys a chance for the spot of head-chef. Francisco's stubbornness wasted this opportunity for change.

Apply fitting ability in the fitting place.

Japanese proverb

Something totally different happened at Finn McCool's, a family pub annex restaurant in the Hamptons. Buddy, the owner, opened this pub after he retired from the police force. Both of his sons work at the restaurant. Jason is the bar manager and Brian is the chef. There is enormous tension between Brian on the one hand and father Buddy and Jason on the other. Buddy tells us that Brian is very arrogant and cuts corners. His nickname is "Chef Shortcut." Brian thinks that it is impossible to work with his family. When pressure mounts on Brian, who is not an experienced cook, Brian flips and leaves the restaurant. With no one in the kitchen, Gordon says that Buddy has to take over. But Buddy is not up to the task; he screws up orders and drops tableware. He gets quite frustrated and remarks, "No wonder that Brian is a cranky bitch." The next day Brian returns. His family ties turned out to be stronger than his irritation. But by having to take over the role of chef, Buddy and Jason have gained tremendous respect for the hard work that Brian has to put in every day and they realize that they have to value Brian much more.

Almost all organizations claim that they value their employees. But perhaps the more fascinating question is how to determine the 'fair value' of employees. Interesting in this respect are recent studies on inequity aversion; i.e. our ingrained human preference for fairness. Various studies have shown that perceived fairness with respect to pay and performance is extremely important for the performance of teams and businesses (Chan Kim & Mauborgne, 1997). If employees sense unfair dealings this quickly leads to envy, low morale, and outright resistance. This human preference for fairness is probably deep-rooted in our DNA. In an experiment with capuchin monkeys, Sarah Brosnan and Frans de Waal (2003) showed that monkeys prefer receiving nothing to receiving a reward awarded inequitably in favor of a second monkey. For example, if one monkey received a strawberry for a certain task, and another monkey got a cucumber (considered inferior to a strawberry) for the same task, this resulted in anger and irritation with the researchers for the inequitable distribution of food. The monkeys simply refused to take the cucumber out of anger. They preferred not to receive anything, than to get less than another monkey for the same task.

Lately large companies are recognizing how important it is to reward fair value to customers. More and more multinationals are building an Employee Value Proposition (EVP) which says what you may expect from your employer and your job. It is basically the answer to the employee's questions: "What's in it for me?" and "What more can you offer?" (Minchington, 2005). In general there are five elements that a company 'promises' an employee; money, benefits, challenging & interesting work, career opportunities and a feeling of belongingness. Companies such as AstraZeneca are investing in an Employee Value Proposition to attract talent and to ensure that the mutual expectations of employer and employee are clear.

Change Principle 17: Communicate to the Soul

At La Riviera (Inverness, Scotland), the cooking of head chef Loic is simply too complex. A young, ambitious, and talented chef of 28 years of age, he is anxious to create new innovative dishes that will bring him instant recognition. But as a result Loic's dishes are too complicated. Gordon Ramsay is unable to convince stubborn head-chef Loic and owner Barry that by refusing to trust the flown-in, high-quality and fresh ingredients not only puts off his customers, but can turn off potential Michelin inspectors. After two days of heavy arguments, Gordon Ramsay invites owner Barry into the restaurants bar. "Recommend me a whisky," Gordon instructs the bartender and orders one for Barry as well. After the bartender has poured two glasses with the finest whisky, Gordon asks him, "Can I have a touch of soda in there, please." The bartender explains that he cannot do this, because it will spoil the whisky. "Are you suggesting or telling me," Gordon asks the bartender. "Doing both," he replies and explains that there is no way he will combine soda with a malt whisky, "There is no way." Gordon explains that he is absolutely right, and adds "You don't f**k with things that are good." Gordon explains: "When you have got quality ingredients, you let them speak for themselves."

Gordon uses this simple example to show Loic and Barry that the food is too complicated, but for the past two days his message was constantly declined. Gordon tried another technique. He invited an acclaimed Michelin critic to taste Loic' food. This critic gave the same message to Loic (i.e. your dishes are too complicated), but Loic remained in denial.. Only when the communication became very tangible with the whisky as a strong example, was Gordon able to convince the owner and chef.

This example demonstrates the value in effective communication rather than merely focusing on the message itself. To communicate effectively, sometimes new channels of communication have to be found in order to get the message across to the recipient. In (turnaround) management, communication plays a key role. This is, however, not easy, as the restaurant's failure and required changes produce uncertainty and anxiety, triggering strong emotional responses and resistance that stand in the way of effective communication (i.e., an exchange of information). Simply telling what they should or should not do simply does not work in this kind of situation, and a different approach is necessary. What is required is a removal of emotions during communication, which enables the information to be exchanged. This avoids merely expressing one's frustration regarding a person or situation. There are several ways to accomplish this task. For example at D-place, Gordon comments about the fact that head-chef Philippe and maître d Dave are not communicating with one another, "The animosity between Dave and Philippe is dragging the business down. They are like a bickering old couple.

It's time to start building bridges, with some tried and tested marriage guidance tactics."
Gordon takes them apart, and says to Philippe, "Hold out your hand," and puts an egg
in his hand. Gordon explains that he is only allowed to talk when he is holding the eggs,
and that he has to tell Dave what he really thinks about him. "Well Dave, you are just
an arrogant little bastard." Philippe lashes at Dave. Now Dave gets a change to get it of
his chest and says, "I think you are talking out of your ass, because if I do talk to you,
and shout, it is because you argue and don't let me finish. So, from now on, stop being
a stubborn French bastard." Later on, the communication civilizes and becomes less
personal and more about work. Then Gordon explains that this exercise is not
personal, but about business and about doing your f**king jobs. "I just beg you both to
continue talking to one another, cause that hasn't taken place. Understand each other's
jobs." Finally, Gordon has them shake hands.

In the example above, Gordon provides Dave and Philippe with the opportunity to get
it of their chest, and tell the other what has been bothering them all this time. This
releases the emotional tension between them, after which more effective
communication becomes possible. Another way to diffuse the situation is to frame the
problem within a different context. This can be done verbally via use of analogies and
metaphors, while games can be used to provide people with an actual experience.

Games are often used by Gordon to facilitate communication between staff members
or to get his point across. At Campania, after introducing the new menu, Gordon wants
to motivate the waiters and waitresses and decides to have a little contest. The first to
sell all the items on the menu wins the contest and earns one hundred dollars. Besides
motivating front-of-house staff, it also teaches them a valuable lesson about how order-

taking can be used to influence the flow in the kitchen. At Capri, Gordon takes the twin owners to a boxing gym and instructs them to let go of their frustration while sparring with Gordon and with each other. During the training session, one of the twins confesses to Gordon that he thinks that he is a failure. "You are not a failure. We all make mistakes in life. Embrace change," Gordon explains and asks, "Are you keen to make this business work?" With this simple exercise, the twins are able to release their frustration and let down their guards. This enables Gordon to really get through to them, and to convince them to embrace change. At Oscar's, Gordon starts a competition with Lenny to get him to quit smoking during service, by putting a pound in a box every time Lenny goes out for a smoke, while Gordon has to do the same every time he curses. During a fishing trip at the Sandgate Hotel, Gordon suggests a little communication game. Every time someone catches a fish, he has to share something with the group about what he actually thinks about the restaurant. Gordon comments: "team spirit is vital to a good kitchen."

Nothing that is worth knowing can be taught.

Oscar Wilde

In the Curry Lounge, Gordon needs to convince the staff of the absurdity of the menu, which contains a ridiculous amount of variation. The extreme combination of flavors in effect lead to dishes that all taste the same. To show this to the staff Gordon decides to order every dish on the menu, and to have the staff taste them blindly to spot the differences between them. Naturally, they cannot taste the differences between the dishes. Only after this exercise are they themselves convinced of the absurdity of the menu.

If we are able to provide people with an actual experience, it makes them aware of the point that we want to make. This is basically a process of taking meaning from direct experience (i.e., learning through reflection on doing), and is also known as experiential learning. Aristotle once said, "For the things we have to learn before we can do them, we learn by doing them" (Bynam and Porter, 2005: 9). In this sense, Gordon acts both as a process consultant (i.e., a type of consultant who acts as a facilitator to help individuals and groups deal with issues of process, rather than task; this is especially the case in the UK series), and as an expert consultant (i.e., a professional that provides expert advice).

A great marketing example of the power of experience can be found at General Electric. At the Farnborough airshow GE hired holographic projection specialist Musion Systems to create a 3D holographic jet engine. Members of the public could go on stage to assemble the engine virtually to get an experience of the expertise of GE's engineers. There are more great examples of the power of holograms such as the amazed music fans at the Coachella 2012 rock festival in California when a hologram of murdered rap star Tupac Shakur was projected at the festival, which then performed with real life rappers Snoop Dogg and Dr Dre for 15 minutes.

V. CHANGE

To continue with our medical analogy, after the patient has accepted and taken responsibility for the disease, treatment can begin. Obviously, the precise treatment depends upon the seriousness of the disease, and ranges from a simple band aid, to taking medicine, undergoing surgery, or intensive care. Regarding the treatment of disease, the following Dutch saying applies, "lenient healers make stinking wounds." This means that half measures will only worsen the ailment, and not eradicate it. For this reason, doctors will tend to "use a cannon to kill a mosquito," to make sure that the disease is completely eradicated.

The same principle applies to organizational change, and half measures need to be avoided at all cost. As the doctor first addresses the illness that is most fatal, a change manager first needs to tackle the issue that is fatal for the restaurant. This is exactly what goes wrong in many change initiatives. They tend to focus on quick wins and forget the big issues (see change principle # 21).

In practice this means going against the practice of many 'so-called' change or turnaround managers, who often follow a simple step-by-step change process (e.g., Kotter's (1996) eight-stage process, or the Kanter's (1992) Ten Commandments). In these processes, it is often recommended to aim for the low hanging fruit or short-term wins first. While we do not deny the importance of short term gains in any change process, the big issue should always be given top priority. After all, in a situation of life and death, no doctor would risk a patient's life by wasting time to provide the patient with a temporary relief. Instead, the doctor would only concentrate on what contributes to the patient's survival chances, and afterwards concern himself with lesser matters.

In an organizational turnaround (i.e., after overt failure of the organization and faulty action taken by management), going for the low hanging fruit without addressing the big issue actually sends the wrong signal to the organization, because staff members interpret this signal that probably nothing significant will actually change. As previously explained, the cause of failure always lies at the management of the organization. However, due to their unconscious denial, they are unaware of their own failure. Instead, they blame other organizational members for the organization's crisis, and consistently take the wrong actions to combat failure. Being less emotionally involved in the whole situation, organizational members at the lower ranks often suffer less from unconscious denial, and are better able to see what is exactly wrong with the organization. When telling management however, they are publicly humiliated, as management categorizes this their behaviour as deviant and non-cooperative. After a while, organizational members give up, as any change initiative involves upsetting daily routines and stops members from performing their job as usual while working around the elephant in the room (i.e., management's incompetence). Furthermore, as they will eventually be blamed for the failure of any structural improvement to the organization members they become resistant to change, and extremely sceptical towards management. Hence, it is unsurprising that most employees will adopt a 'wait and see' approach by not committing to the change until they receive clears signals from management that the change is actually beneficial. As most turnaround managers are considered the 'hired guns' of senior management, they too are subject to scepticism. As such, the pursuit of quick wins by the turnaround manager will be viewed negatively. The turnaround manager will be seen as someone who is not tackling the big issues, but as someone who is there only for senior management and his own career. The fact that consultant are hired and fired by management further complicates this matter, as all of them exist by the grace of their employers, and thus, as a general rule, do not bite the hand that feeds them. In such a situation, the turnaround manager needs to send out a clear signal to the staff that this time the change initiative will be different. The turnaround manager needs to publicly tackle the big issues from the start, and go for the root cause of failure – i.e., management.

It is without doubt that quick wins can support the turnaround. For example, in Kitchen Nightmares, Gordon tends to start a turnaround by identifying and confronting the big issues. However, big issues take time to resolve. While Gordon tries to understand the big issues, he also proposes other changes at the same time. Gordon's extensive knowledge of cooking and the restaurant business comes into play. Gordon is creative in finding new recipes, possesses great market orientation, and has extensive experience with all aspects of running a restaurant. These abilities are not sufficient to make him a great turnaround manager, but are of crucial importance in the initial phases of the change process. His vast knowledge of restaurants means that he is able to identify and implement quick wins quickly. And, this enables Gordon to avoid significant resistance to the proposed changes while raising the probability of a successful turnaround.

Change Principle 18: Ignite the Passion

Danielle is the 21-year old head chef of Hot Potato Café, a restaurant in the suburbs of Philadelphia. Danielle does not really want to be a chef. She is there to help out here older nieces who own the place and cannot afford a proper chef. On the first day of the turnaround Gordon Ramsay observes that there are no potato dishes on the menu. A little bit strange for a restaurant called Hot Potato Café. On the second day Gordon asks the three sisters and chef Danielle to create with a new potato dish ("let's do something new, something exiting, let's do something together"). Danielle's newly created dish is delicious. With this new dish she demonstrates that she has a real talent for cooking. Gordon recognizes Danielle's talent and hires a mentor for her (Richard Marsh). At the end of the show Danielle says: "cooking was not a big aspiration, but it changed 360. This is the career that I want." By supporting Danielle and recognizing her talents Gordon ignited her passion for cooking.

Another example where Gordon revamped the passion for cooking can be found in the episode on The Curry Lounge. The food in this restaurant was tasteless. But Gordon was genuinely convinced that Indian chef Khan could cook. Gordon takes Khan to the local food market. At the market he casually asks Khan where his cooking influences came from. Khan replied, his mother who inspired him with her style inherited from the Indian mountains. Gordon suggests creating a special dish to put on the menu based on his mother's recipes. This special is then placed on the menu and Khan explains the dish to the front of house staff. Through this simple intervention Khan reignites his passion for cooking and at the end of the show, The Curry Lounge is no longer an ordinary Indian restaurant. Within a mile radius 18 other Indian restaurants also compete for custom. However, The Curry Lounge now has a passionate chef at the helm with original dishes from the mountainous region of India.

We have seen at the beginning of this book that passion is essential for the success of any restaurant, or business (see X-factor # 1). As Gordon explains in The Priory, "to succeed, you must have passion." If the passion and love for food have gone, staff will start to cut corners, become lazy, and the rot sets in. To avoid impending doom, passion must be reinstated. We have already explained that it starts from the top, with the owner of the restaurant, as it is his/her responsibility to make sure that the kitchen and dining room are run by passionate people, and they set the standard for the rest of the staff. But the most important person in this equation is probably the head chef, because, as Gordon explains in La Parra de Burriana, "good food will sell itself." Even if a restaurant sucks at everything else, if the food is great, customers will come back. A turnaround manager should focus on reigniting the passion of the head chef, but this is not straightforward.

One technique used to reignite the passion for cooking is to reconnect with cooking ingredients (e.g., Gordon takes the kitchen staff from the Priory to a cow expert, goes tomato picking with Mike from Fish and Anchor, and visits a vegetable farm with the staff from The Granary), or by installing new equipment that can be used in the cooking process (e.g., in Sushi-Ko, where Gordon installs a whole new kitchen for Akira). A second technique that can be used to make chefs passionate again is to have them cooking again from within, which is accomplished by asking the chef to produce a favourite dish and one that makes the chef feel proud. This implies that the head chef should be responsible for the menu to ensure that the dishes included are ones he feels passionate about.. There is nothing more frustrating to a head chef than having to cook dishes because he is ordered to. Chefs are creative people who want to express themselves through their work (cooking/ dishes). If chef's lose their passion, and stop caring about the food, basic hygiene standards quickly slip. A third possibility is to chefs cook for important people, like family (Oscar's), influential people/celebrities (e.g., The Priory), and food critics (e.g., La Riviera, the Secret Garden). Sometimes, just having people spend more time in the kitchen, preparing food can reignite their passion (e.g., La Lanterna). Obviously, cooking alongside a top chef like Gordon provides a once in a lifetime opportunity that many chefs do not want to miss out on (e.g., La Gondola).

Merely reintroducing a chef to the kitchen environment may not be enough to reignite a passion for cooking. This is one of the reasons for Gordon's provocative approach, so that he can redirect the anger and frustration chef's/owners express and turn it into positive energy. In what can be referred to as counselling, Gordon tries to change the perspective that people have of themselves and the world. For example, in Sabiatello's,

Gordon uses a picture show cataloguing Sammy's life which helps him to reconnect with the passion for cooking he experienced in his youth. In La Parra de Burriana, Gordon ignites the owner's passion by asking him how proud he would feel when the restaurant failed, and he would return to the UK with his dick between his legs. In The Curry Lounge, Gordon restored the chef's passion by asking him to talk about his inspiration for cooking.

Nothing great in the world has ever been accomplished without passion.

Georg Wilhelm Friedrich Hegel

One of the greatest US business leaders of all time is perhaps Charles Michael Schwab (18 February 1862 – 18 October 1939), the first CEO with a yearly income of over a million dollars. Under his guidance Bethlehem Steel became one of largest steel makers in the world. Schwab's ways of dealing with his employees are aptly described in Dale Carnegie's (1936) celebrated book: How to Win Friends and Influence People. From Carnegie's book we have taken an anecdote about how Charles Schwab motivated his workers. The story goes as follows: Charles Schwab had a steel mill manager whose people weren't delivering their quota of work. *"How is it,"* Schwab asked him, "that a manager as capable as you can't make this mill turn out what it should?" "I don't know," the manager replied. "I've coaxed the men, I've pushed them, I've sworn and cussed, I've threatened them with damnation and being fired. But nothing works. They just won't produce." This conversation took place at the end of the day, just before the night shift came on. Schwab asked the manager for a piece of chalk, then, turning to the nearest man, asked: "How many heats did your shift make today?" "Six." Without another word, Schwab chalked a big figure six on the floor, and walked away. When the night shift came in, they saw the "6" and asked what it meant.   "The big boss was in here today," the day people said. "He asked us how many heats we made, and we told him six. He chalked it down on the floor." The next morning Schwab walked through the mill again. The night shift had rubbed out "6" and replaced it with a big "7." When the day shift reported for work the next morning, they saw a big "7" chalked on the floor. So the night shift thought they were better than the day shift did they? Well, they would show the night shift a thing or two. The crew pitched in with enthusiasm, and when they quit that night, they left behind them an enormous, swaggering "10." Things were stepping up. Shortly this mill, which had been lagging way behind in production, was turning out more work than any other mill in the plant.

Charles Schwab himself said that he was paid this salary largely because of his ability to deal with people and to arouse enthusiasm. "The way to get things done," says Schwab, "is to stimulate competition. I do not mean in a sordid, money-getting way, but in the desire to excel." This is exactly what Gordon Ramsay does in the chefs and owners who win his trust. He stimulates them and encourages individuals to excel in their trade, be it owner, chef or maître-d.

Change Principle 19: Tough Love

The Fish and Anchor is a restaurant based in Lampeter, rural West Wales which
is owned and run by ex-boxer Mike and his wife Caron. Mike is a former 'Fish and
Chips' cook who has won 700,000 pounds at the lottery. From this winnings Mike has
bought his dream come true; a proper restaurant, his Michelin star dream.
Unfortunately, Mike is not such a great cook. He has bought a whole pile of cookbooks
to increase his cooking knowledge and abilities. After watching dinner service ("21
people are cooked for, it looked 201 people"), Gordon starts the second day with the
words: "Time for a bit of tough love." Then he forces Mike to give all his beloved cook
books to charity. This is quite a shock to Mike as his self-esteem and confidence are
largely based on the possession of these cookbooks. But Gordon Ramsay carefully
explains why he forces Mike to get rid of his beloved books: "Mike is attempting to be
someone that he is not. To help him I need to find the real Mike." When the books are

brought to charity, Gordon takes Mike to a local farm and shows him the sweetest tomatoes. Gordon starts to teach Mike the quality of different ingredients. Next Gordon takes Mike into the kitchen and teaches him slowly how to cook from his heart using the finest ingredients bought at the local farm. He thereby focuses on Italian dishes as Gordon discovers that Mike has an Italian heritage on which he is very proud. The Italian heritage then becomes one of the pillars on which Gordon shapes Mike's new identity to rebuild his confidence.

The above example demonstrates the most commonly used technique by Gordon in Kitchen Nightmares. On the one hand Gordon is confrontational and not afraid to be brutally honest, even blunt. He is also prepared to physically fight for his opinion. He shakes people out of their comfort zone. But, crucially, a second later he is capable of demonstrating affection and support in order to rebuild individuals and organizations. However, if Gordon stopped at removing people's comfort zones without providing guidance and support, the resulting change in behaviour would be short-lived. It is the combination of breaking the old habits and quickly replacing it with new behaviour that is crucial to organizational change. In short, 'tough love' (or the stick and the carrot) is absolutely essential to change.

Another example of tough love can be found in the same episode; The Fish and Anchor. At a certain moment Gordon is arguing with Carol. Then Gordon suddenly asks: "Is this a competition between you and me?" and immediately thereafter says: "Please calm down and let me help." He constantly reminds the subjects of change (e.g. Carol) that he is there for them, so they can survive. Every episode is full of these 'tough love' examples. In the same episode Gordon invents a game where actresses pose as mock clients so the waitresses can learn how to create a welcoming atmosphere. He then says: "I am testing you all, not to make you look stupid, but to make the service friendlier". Gordon constantly reminds the owners and staff that he is there to help.

The help and support of Gordon goes beyond practical and effective advice. In many of the restaurants he is not afraid to help out refurbishing the restaurant or cleaning the kitchen. This empathetic behaviour is sometimes crucial to the change which can be deduced from the episode on Finn McCool's. Gordon helps by scrubbing the kitchen. Brian, chef and son of owner Buddy, found this help most impressive. Seeing Gordon, the great chef, cleaning his kitchen altered his ego and lowered his resistance. The 'love' aspect of Gordon cannot be denied and is effectively used to breakdown the remaining resistance.

Gordon's active help goes beyond what you might expected of this brutal blasphemous chef as demonstrated in the Piccolo Teatro where owner Rachel runs a vegetarian restaurant in the middle of Paris. The restaurant loses 5,500 Euros per month. Although it is notoriously difficult to own a vegetarian restaurant in Paris, the restaurant occupies a prime location. Gordon is therefore amazed that Rachel does not open for lunch. To convince her that this is a serious mistake, Gordon secretly opens for lunch, sets a big sign outside the restaurant and does the cooking (soup) and serving, by himself, running around from kitchen to customers and vice versa. 'I do not even work this hard in my own restaurant." During lunch the restaurant makes almost 450 Euros in less than two hours demonstrating to Rachel that not opening for lunch is a costly mistake. Such support clearly goes beyond what you may expect from a turnaround manager.

Of course, Gordon has good reason to be so sympathetic. His unexpected kindheartedness, after his provocative behaviour, is essential in creating a strong bond with the owner and staff. It creates a shared feeling that: "we are on the same page." Besides showing benevolent behaviour, Gordon uses techniques to reinforce the impression of a strong bond. He is humble, direct, open, looks for eye contact and demonstrates humour and empathy. Moreover, Gordon is a master in matching (a.k.a. mirroring) individuals to create (the impression of) strong bonds. There are various ways to match or mirror someone. You can match someone's experience, goals, vision, hobbies, body language, et cetera. In all episodes there are clear examples of Gordon "mirroring" key individuals. In the case of Lenin, the alcoholic chef at Oscar's, Gordon is open about the fact that his own father was an alcoholic. To Loic and the staff of La Riviera, the posh restaurant in Scotland, he was honest about his failed attempts to open a stylish restaurant in Glasgow. In Davide, the classic Italian restaurant in Boston where owner Frank was cheated by his brother and co-owner Anthony, Gordon was candid about the drug addiction of his Brother.

Gordon is a genuinely charming person and can develop a good rapport with most people. But the great skill of Gordon is that he only builds rapport when he thinks this bond is beneficial to the turnaround. Therefore, at the beginning of a turnaround, when Gordon first meets the owners and kitchen staff, he will actively destroy any level of rapport. He engages in a kind of emotional dance to sometimes build rapport and subsequently disengage. In the outset of a turnaround it is imperative that the owner and/or chef does not feel too secure. Only when the subject of change realizes that he or she needs to change and they are no longer comfortable, can Gordon decide whether they are committed to changing and only then, does rapport commence. From that moment onwards they accepted the change and can start to feel safe while sensing that they are able to trust Gordon.

The standard approach adopted by Gordon is to be sincere in both his words and deeds. But there is one thing that is always clear: He is not there for his own ego. Gordon is there to help. In Rococo Gordon tells owner Nick: "I think you can do better with half the thrills, I am here to help." Then Nicks asks: "Is nothing OK?" Gordon: "I would not be here." Gordon is like a parent to his drug addicted son: "I will help you, if you stay off the drugs." He shows true love, but this love is not unconditionally.

Tough love has become standard practice when dealing with addicts. Friends and families are encouraged to take a stern attitude towards a relative or friend suffering from an addiction in order to help them recover. The 'tough love approach' has been widely used between parents and addicted children who are sometimes forced to attend "boot camps," "emotional-growth centers," and "behaviour-modification programs." Although the results of these approaches are mixed, it is clear that tough treatment alone simply does not work. This toughness has to be combined with love. The importance of love and support is also an important feature of Alcoholics Anonymous (AA) where addicts are supported by a group and not judged on their behaviour.

Venture-capitalists, incubators and programs such as start-up DNA are business examples of tough love. These investors and business partners are willing to support a young start-up firm, but in return the entrepreneur has to be able to talk the talk and walk the walk. And the questions of these potential investors are often quite tough. But when these investors such as Draper Fisher Jurvetson finally invest they often support the young entrepreneurs not only with sufficient funds, but also with good advice and great networks. The bottom line is that we all need some tough-love when growing, even as grown-ups.

Change Principle 20: Treat the Cause not the Symptom

The key to a successful turnaround is always in the hands of the owner of the restaurant. But in most cases, this is here where the biggest problem lies; the owner is in denial of the problem, or is simply unwilling to change. In Peter's Restaurant in Babylon, New York, the real problem is obvious; his name is Peter and he is the co-owner of the family-owned Italian establishment. Although Peter is manager by name, in practice he does not do anything except take care of his ego. According to Peter, he is more important than the deteriorating restaurant: "I take care of myself and it shows. Instead of a stove, I bought a suit." Peter drives a big Mercedes and is more proud of this car than his restaurant. Peter gives away free meals, is a tyrant to his staff, and takes money out of the till even though the family restaurant is losing money. He even eats the food that is prepared and intended for customers. No wonder that his sister and co-owner, Tina, is stressed out. Peter portrays himself as an immense and impressive individual, but according to the kitchen staff, Peter is no more than a 250-pound baby. He is a very violent and quick tempered man. For example, when one of the restaurant suppliers visits the restaurant to collect an outstanding debt, Peter starts fighting with this much smaller man, effectively embarrassing his father and driving away any of the remaining customers. In short; people are afraid to stand up to Peter as he is an aggressive 250-pound bully.

To turn the restaurant around, Gordon says that he wants to create a true family restaurant ("The definition of a true family restaurant is that every member of the family is working in it to make it a success"). This is a smart move by Gordon as this definition of a "real" family restaurant does not only give a shared and tangible vision to the restaurant to all concerned, but implies a change in the behaviour of big boy Peter. He needs to start making a contribution. Gordon says that Peter will need to start working in the kitchen. He will actually cook the food. Tina and her mom will run the dining room. Peter is soon aggravated by the work and can't handle the pressure. He demands an orange juice. Gordon tells him to go f**k himself. Peter is shocked. But the kitchen staff is delighted; "Finally someone told him, do not act like the king over here' cause buddy you have got nothing." After dinner Gordon bluntly states that Peter is the problem. Peter then says that he has other problems to deal with. Gordon: "We all got problems. [Gordon points to different people], problem, problem, problem. That is no excuse. You are the only one not pulling your weight and that is not good enough. This place would run better without you." Then Gordon sends the staff away to have a two minute personal chat with Peter. He tells Peter to go home and come back tomorrow. "Think about what you can bring into this business. Make sure it is damn good, because I am here to check upon it." Peter sleeps over it and then comes to his senses. Peter: "I am hurt. Gordon has said things to me that other people are wanting to say but have not said that to me." The next day, Peter is at work early and is actually helping.

The example above demonstrates a couple of important points about organizational change. First, you should never be afraid to say what you need to say. Peter's ill-tempered character combined with his size prevented many people from speaking up. Courage is imperative in organizational change. Second, you cannot solve minor issues in an organization if you are not prepared to tackle the big issues. In most big organizations there are powerful tyrants like Peter, perhaps they operate more subtly, but tyrants nonetheless. If you do not confront these people, but instead focus on the low hanging fruit, nothing will really change. Third, the big issues can often be found in the top of the organization. In a failing restaurant the owner or the chef are usually the biggest problems. Similarly, in a failing organization the directors and managers are equally at fault.

Publicly correcting the owner is the most important lever a turnaround manager has. It is very visible and sends a strong message to both owner and staff; the buck stops here. It is one of the crucial interventions of a turnaround manager, and also one of the most risky; it may be the end of your job. That is perhaps the reason why this type of intervention is rarely used in practice. Many turnaround managers lack the guts or the mandate to really rectify the behaviour of the top dog (owner, chef, CEO, or whoever).

Extreme remedies are appropriate for extreme diseases.

Hippocrates

Correcting an owner or executive is not that easy. A case in point is made by Paul Babiak (2006). According to Babiak, one in 25 bosses is a psychopath; this rate is four times higher than the percentage psychopaths in the general population. Psychopaths thrive on their charm and manipulative powers which sometimes is easily mistaken for leadership. Psychopaths are characterized by being completely amoral and concerned with their own power and desires. Evidently, the large majority of bosses are not psychopaths. But it is certainly unlikely that a boss does not possess some narcissistic elements, which is another well-known trait in leaders. These bosses tend to become easily upset by any criticism. In both cases the boss, psychopath or narcissist, is not easily corrected or convinced of the greater good. And even if the boss is quite a ordinary person, it is wise to keep in mind that nobody likes to be criticized.

A wonderful example a psychopathic CEO is "Chainsaw Al" Dunlap. As a CEO he "rescued" a series of companies (e.g. American Can, Lily Tulip, Crown Zellerbach). In each case brought in C. Donald Burnett of Coopers & Lybrand to work out the details of the vast payroll cuts and plant closings. In 1994, he started as the CEO of Scott paper. On his first day, he invested $2 million of his own money in the business to show his confidence that the company could be turned around and offered three of his former associates top jobs within the company. On the second day, he disbanded the powerful management committee and on the third day, he fired nine of the eleven highest ranking executives. In 1995, Al Dunlap sold Scott Paper to Kimberly-Clark in 1995 for $7.8 billion and walked away with a $100 million golden parachute. This example shows vividly the courage one should have when arguing against a psychopathic CEO or business owner. This is nevertheless crucial when you really want to turn the business around.

Change Principle 21: Fast Follow-up

Brian, the owner and chef at The Fenwick Arms, scares the customers away with his lousy cooking and strange ideas about menus and cutlery. To solve this problem, Gordon bans Brian from the kitchen, and the restaurant starts to flourish. However, Brian still sneaks into the kitchen to influence the staff, and Gordon realizes that he needs a more drastic and structural approach, he needs to find a new role for Brian. Luckily Gordon has an idea; a new role based on Brian's emotions. Brian is an ardent supporter of traditional cooking with English gravy. Gordon, although he is not fond of Brian's gravy ('it looks like tarmac') recognizes the potential of traditional cooking and delicious gravy for the pub. So he creates a new style of gravy with the sous-chefs and says to Brian: "The penny dropped for me today: this restaurant could be famous for gravy." Brian responses: "Brilliant idea." Gordon: You've got the amazing potential to have a fantastic Sunday-Lunch. Bring back real gravy." So Brian's wife asks how. Then Gordon jumps up, takes off his white chef uniform and shows a t-shirt which says "Campaign for real gravy." Subsequently, he grabs a megaphone and says: "you have got a campaign to launch; real gravy. Why can't you get out with the team on the street and spread the word?" Before Brian understands what is happening, he is on the campaign trail with a bus, carrying a megaphone and supported by a team waving flags, spreading the word of "real gravy." Within 12 hours Gordon created a new strategy for the restaurant and a new role for Brian (campaign manager). This campaign is in instant success in bringing new customers and money. Brian does not revert to his old behaviour, and finally accepts the changes. Gordon's direct and rapid action which brings instant success and prevents the re-emergence of negative obsessions.

In Kitchen Nightmares, Gordon applies the principle of direct action on many occasions. For example, in the episode on Rococo, owner Nick is a former Michelin star winner, who is living in the past by trying to hold on to the menu and dishes that brought him his glory days. Nick needs to embrace change, and Gordon decides to have a cook off, where each of them has to make a new dish that will create money. What starts as a game (who can create the finer dish) not only rebuilds the self-confidence of Nick but actually creates a money spinner as the dish is immediately added to the menu. The success of the new dish further restores confidence in Nick as Gordon's action, once again reinforces the virtuous change cycle.

At The Dovecote Bistro, owner Mick promises freshness on the menu, but reheats pre-cooked products bought from a cash-and-carry supermarket. While Gordon is able to convince Mick of the need for fresh ingredients, the credit crunch of 2008 has Mick back at the cash-and-carry in an effort to cut costs. Gordon tries to convince Mick about the need to buy fresh produce locally, to keep the money in the local community.

Gordon explains "if you support the locals, they will support you." Mick is not convinced. On the spur of the moment, Gordon organizes a town meeting. He invites various local customers and suppliers and asks them what they would want from a local restaurant such as the Dovecote Bistro. The locals explain: "local produce, well cooked, 8-9 pounds for a main meal." Again this example shows the importance of direct action. While Mick is initially not convinced of the idea of local sourcing, the speedy assembly of local customers and suppliers underpins Gordon's thinking and removes Mick's remaining resistance. The direct action enables Gordon to go to the next step; executing a new sourcing strategy.

The most drastic, and usually the most effective remedy for fear is direct action.

William Burnham

Direct action can be extremely important for several reasons. First, it results in an immediate change of behaviour, with no room for postponement. This implies that people do not have the opportunity to find reasons to resist the change because they do not want to face the uncertainty and anxiety that the change produces, which minimizes the resistance to change. Second, through a process called backward rationalization, people rationalize their behaviour after it has occurred, which means that they look for rational reasons to explain their actions after the fact. Thus, if you get people to behave in the way you want them to, they will find their own reasons of why they did so later. Hence, they will accept and validate the change merely because they have changed. The importance of direct action is very visible in judo economics; a strategy that enables a small company to challenge a large multinational corporation with the help of agility and movement. Judo strategy begins with movement. Here quickness and agility are used to win markets. Fast follow up is essential to maintain the initial lead. A great example of a company that has demonstrated this judo technique in the past is Austrian brand Red Bull. Due to its focus (i.e., one drink, limited number of vendors, hip, cool, and colourful customers, extreme sports marketing) in combination with its fast execution Red Bull has been able to maintain its lead over the competition since the late 1980s, despite the power of the mega soft-drink companies such as PepsiCo and Coca-Cola. If a company is able to implement changes rapidly, it can leave the competition in its wake.

Change Principle 22: Teach your Children well

Nigel, the 46 year old owner and chef of Clubway 41, one of the 650 restaurants in touristic Blackpool, cannot cook. He is not the only chef without real cooking capabilities. Gordon: "I am always amazed how many small restaurants have the wrong people in the kitchen." Luckily, cooking does not have to be complicated, as Gordon shows in Piccolo Teatro in Paris: "Cooking at this level is not difficult." One of Gordon's actions is to create dishes which are so simple that even inexperienced and talentless chefs are capable of cooking. He does this by streamlining dishes and simplifying the preparation (X-factor 8). For Nigel, he creates a new recipe for broccoli soup which consists of three cheap ingredients, where the original recipe had 16 expensive ones. Moreover, Gordon creates a fool proof menu for Nigel, which solely consists of dishes that can be prepared in advance. He does something comparable for chef Stuart of The Sandgate Hotel where the original Seabass recipe with 50 ingredients is simplified to a 5 ingredient version. There are more reasons for simplification than simply minimizing the chances of failure and increasing the speed of delivery. In Gordon's own words: "I need to simplify everything, so the rest can spark." Perhaps the most extreme example of simplification can be found in the episode on Moore Place, where owners Mick and Richard have become greedy and have sold 181 seats on Mothers' day. This is overly ambitious for a kitchen staff that cannot fry deep-fried food. Gordon comes up with a plan; He wants Moore Place to serve roast chicken as a special. Clearly, this makes the task for the service staff harder as they have to sell this special in enormous quantities to take the weight off the shoulders of the kitchen staff.

After simplification of the menu, the next step is to educate and train staff. For every level of cooking an appropriate training program can be put in place. As Gordon is an expert cook he is able to find cooking challenges for every level. For instance, in Michelin star restaurant La Riviera Gordon invents the oxtail challenge where the kitchen staff is asked to make something exquisite from a cheap ingredient (an oxtail). This enables Gordon to discover any hidden talent in the kitchen. A comparable, but less demanding assignment is given to the young chefs of the Granary. They have to make a salad using Hampshire root vegetables. Not only does Gordon himself taste the salad, but he also lets customers taste them. The best salad will go on the menu, giving young chefs a chance to shine.

Teaching, coaching, and testing of kitchen staff is a standard element in Gordon's approach. Training is perhaps the most frequently used lever of change. Often the training of kitchen staff starts with one or two specials, but soon staff members need to be able to prepare and cook a whole new menu. Obviously, they have to be trained in these dishes, before they are able to run a successful service themselves and perform under pressure.

The focus of teaching is not always on the quality of food. It can be on every aspect of cooking such as creating dishes and communicating with the staff. For instance, in Bazzini (the restaurant in Ridgewood, New Jersey) Gordon devised a training exercise to test chef Paul Bazzini's cooking under pressure. He unexpectedly tells Paul that he has fifteen minutes to make him a good pasta dish. The timer has already started. Go! Without distractions, Paul suddenly got into the zone and serves the dish on time. In the case of Lenin Mooris, the chef of Oscars, Gordon gives him a strict budget, and for this budget Lenin has to buy all his ingredients. Although both Lenin and Paul can cook, being a good chef is about much more than cooking and these exercises are designed to train these supplementary skills.

Front-of-house staff is also regularly trained in new behaviour and skills. In Moore Place, service staff is taught how to properly slice roasted chicken. In the Fish and Anchor, Gordon gives staff lessons in order taking where he uses actresses to act as mock clients. Even owners are subjected to compulsory training exercises. In The Sandgate Hotel, owner Lois is afraid to discipline staff. First, Gordon makes a Polaroid photo of every staff member. Then he attaches these pictures on various bottles. After that everything is prepared for Lois's assertiveness training; Lois has to tell each person depicted on the bottles what she requires from them as a member of staff. After this dress rehearsal, Lois then has to tell the staff members in person what she needs from them. This exercise is based on the principle that before we are able to do something (i.e., display some kind of behaviour) we need to visualize doing it, and then put the vision into practice.

Education is not the filling of a pail, but the lighting of a fire.

William Butler Yeats

Charita, the owner of Momma Cherri's Soul Food Shack, is another example. She is too soft and does not know how to run a business. As a consequence, there is twice as many staff as need be. Gordon explains that the price of a dish should consist of 1/3 costs of the ingredients, 1/3 staff costs, and 1/3 gross profit. To get his point to really sink in, Gordon and Charita bake two cakes; a cake with the ingredients in the right proportions (1/3, 1/3, 1/3) , and a cake where the proportions are off. Of course, the cake with the disproportionate ingredients looks bad and is tasteless, and the one with the right proportions is delightful and tasty. This exercise seems silly, but is very effective as the message really sinks in with Charita; you cannot have inflated staff costs.

The only sustainable way to stay ahead of one's competitors is to learn faster than they do

Arie de Geus

The importance of learning in business can perhaps be best understood from the notion of the continuous learning organization; a concept largely developed by Peter Senge in his book The Fifth Discipline (Senge, 1994). This views organizations as dynamical systems that are continuously adapting to their environments. To really create a learning organization one needs to have more than the ability to execute training. Such an organization should appreciate diversity, be open to ideas, provide time for reflection, collect information, share information, do proper analysis, and educate and train the employees.

Perhaps the best learning organization can be found in the military where failure to learn from past failures will immediately lead to future casualties. The US Army has applied After Action Reviews (AAR's) rigorously to improve its ability to learn from both successes and failures. One of the main drivers for these AAR's was the US experience in the Vietnam war where it became obvious that waiting for a full evaluation report from headquarters would mean waiting far too long. Another vivid example which shows the crucial importance of learning in the military is: "The Army/Marine field Manual on Counterinsurgency." In this manual, General David Petraeus states that the side that learns quickest wins. He calls counterinsurgency a competition of learning between different sides. Promoting learning is thus a key responsibility of all commanders.

Change Principle 23: Laugh

Bonapartes Restaurant is a fine dining restaurant in Yorkshire, England. Bonapartes' problem is that the local citizens are not really interested in fine dining. They think it is snobbish and too expensive. Gordon argues that the restaurant should be turned into a bistro. To test the preferences of the local public Gordon and Chef Tim go around the town with two different dishes; a fine dining dish and a typical Bistro dish. At the end of their trip, when all the food is distributed to the member of the local community, Tim and Gordon slowly walk back towards the restaurant along the river. Then suddenly, out of nowhere, Gordon throws all the expensive silverware in the river. There is no reason for it and it's probably illegal pollution of the river, but it really makes Chef Tim laugh. When something happens that you do not expect to happen, that's often a reason for laughter.

In the introduction, we have already explained that turnaround management produces great deals of stress and tension. Especially the two transitions 1) from being unconsciously incapable to consciously incapable and 2) from being consciously incapable to consciously capable produce a lot of tension. The reason is that the first transition touches at the core of our identity (i.e., we need to admit that we are incapable), and the latter transition confronts us with failure (i.e., we need to learn a new capability step-by-step). If this tension is not properly released, it will create resistance and frustration that reduces the willingness to change and can even lead to explosions. One way to remove this tension is through laughter.

You can't stay mad at somebody who makes you laugh.

Jay Leno

Gordon uses a lot of humour to release tension. This sense of humour makes his communication funnier and even entertaining. For example, Gordon asks "where is my bible" to the staff of La Riviera, in reference to the Sunday church atmosphere at the restaurant. At the Granary, owner Nigel is way too serious, so Gordon has him dress up as a chicken during a community event. This is comical to the staff who enjoy the mockery of an all too serious boss. At Fleming, a Danish Restaurant without Danish owners or chefs, Gordon decides to bring a Danish dictionary, to make sure that he understands what they are saying. At the Spanish Pavilion, Gordon apologizes for being underdressed, in reference to the stiff tuxedos that the waiters are wearing. At Fiesta Sunrise, the owners give away free tequila appetizers, and in reference to the poor quality of food, Gordon comments: "maybe that is the key, get in the restaurant, get drunk on the free tequila, and then enjoy the food." We are not saying that you have to be a stand-up comedian when you are a turnaround manager, but a little mockery, fun, and laughter can be very important. The examples above show that laughter is still one of the best medicines. The art of humour brings in a new perspective, a new way of looking to things, and it creates strong bonds. Laughter gives energy and has the power to do away with irritation and resentment. No turnaround can be successful without it.

Pleasure in the job puts perfection in the work.

Aristotle

Sometimes if you wander around leading businesses today, you wonder where all the playfulness, giggling, laughter, and fun from your childhood days have gone. In most places work is a rational thing where play and laughter are scarce. Have we forgotten how to have fun? Or is there a special reason or business benefit to our seriousness? Evidence seems to suggest this is not the case at all. Rather it is the other way around. Humour, fun, and play at work provide distraction and releases negative energy. A fun work environment raises morale and diminishes interpersonal conflicts. There seems to be every reason to have fun in the workplace.

In their celebrated book Fish! A Proven Way to Boost Morale and Improve Results, writers Stephen Lundin, John Christensen, Harry Paul, and Ken Blanchard (2000) reported on the behaviour at a Seattle fish market that distinguished one sales stand from all the rest; Pike Place Fish market. The employees of this fish stand displayed a cheerful attitude, engaged and welcomed people, made a lot of noise, threw fish back and forth, displayed energy and enthusiasm, and attempted to make the customers' visits memorable. When asked why they did this, one employee said, "Why not choose to be world famous rather than ordinary?" Evidently, the employees of Pike Place understood that having fun makes a difference; not only for employees, but also for customers.

Perhaps the best example of a company that understands that having fun is good for corporate revenues is Southwest Airlines. They want employees to have fun together, treat each other as family and wants teams and employees that fit together. These goals are supported by a variety of operational procedures (e.g. selection, training). Herb Keleher, CEO and co-founder, says: "We want people to do things well, with laughter and grace." The LOVE and KISS strategy of Southwest Airlines has enabled them to generate a profit for the past 39 years while virtually every other major U.S. airline has declared bankruptcy in the past 10 years.

Change Principle 24: Be Creative

Clubway 41 is a 40-seater restaurant above a café in touristic Blackpool. It is owned and run by David Jackson and his partner Dawn Brindley. After Gordon has successfully turned this restaurant around, he returns a couple of months later. He discovers that the restaurant is again struggling because a bus stop has been located just in front of the restaurant. Almost continuously a crowd waits at this bus stop, blocking the restaurant from view. The owners are devastated by this misfortune. They have asked the local council for a relocation of the bus stop, which has been consistently turned down. Owners David and Dawn do not see a way out of this difficult situation. But instead of seeing the bus stop as a problem, Gordon regards the bus stop a major opportunity. Recognizing that these people have to wait for the bus anyway, he creates a fast, very cheap menu that draws in families with children by the dozens. Additionally, he advertises the restaurant on the bus. In this way the bus stop is transformed from a business risk into a valuable asset. This example shows that you sometimes have to think differently.

In x-factor 3 we have seen that the success of any restaurant is determined by the uniqueness of its proposition, especially in a highly competitive environment. While creating a unique proposition sounds relatively easy, there is more to this than meets the eye. After all creating a truly unique selling point is not blatantly obvious. Otherwise, it would not be unique because others would have thought of it as well. Crafting this unique niche requires a lot of creativity and innovative thinking. For instance, at Piccolo Teatro Gordon has the difficult task of creating a competitive edge for a vegetarian food in Paris (where people eat a staggering ninety kilograms of meat per year). Gordon's idea is to match Paris' sexy and indulging atmosphere with equally sexy and indulgent vegetarian food. This is innovative as most vegetarian restaurants are perceived as stuffy and boring.

Creativity is just connecting things. When you ask creative people how they did something, they feel a little guilty because they didn't really do it, they just saw something. It seemed obvious to them after a while. That's because they were able to connect experiences they've had and synthesize new things.

Steve Jobs

The Kitchen Nightmares TV-series provides plenty of cases that vividly demonstrate how one can increase the revenue streams of a restaurant without having to change its core identity and the complete menu. Sometimes relatively small changes can save the business. For example, at The Curry Lounge, the delivery of Tiffin lunchboxes with naan, curry, and rice to nearby office buildings generates a new revenue stream. At J

Willy's, Gordon introduces a unique BBQ sauce that is an instant success and even sold to customers visiting the restaurant. The importance is not to look for the obvious and give room to new ideas, new markets, and new products.

The importance of creativity is well established by now. Research has shown that creative entrepreneurs are more innovative and perform better, especially in rapidly changing markets like the restaurant business. Creativity is often a necessary ingredient of turnarounds as the old way of doing things will probably not take the restaurant much further. But the preconditions for creative thinking, such as trust and openness typically disappear during a turnaround. Especially in a large reorganization, people tend to be very internally focused on details of processes and procedures. It therefore can be very healthy to bring in outside expertise with fresh, creative thinking during such a turnaround.

Recent research has also shown the enormous importance of earlier expertise for innovation. A case in point is James Dyson. His first major invention was the Ballbarrow; a barrow with ball-shaped wheels to use in soft surfaces. Dyson got this idea from his experience in an engineering company where he learned about balloon tyres for amphibious vehicles; a clear case of applying an idea from one field to another. Also his second invention, the Dyson vacuum cleaner, was based on cross-over experiences. Dyson wanted to create a vacuum cleaner based on cyclonic separation. This cyclone idea was not new, but came from the spray-finishing room's air filter in his Ballbarrow factory. Without this earlier experience with the air filter, Dyson would never have made a vacuum cleaner.

Change Principle 25: Give the Right Person the Right Job

Gordon: "The best investment for a restaurant is the chef. He is a major asset in the kitchen, motivator, leader, brings customers back, and gets the best out of his team." Unfortunately, Richard Collins from The Glass House does not belong to this category. Richard is cocky and arrogant, does not take responsibility, is unable to motivate his staff, produces crappy food, and is lazy and clumsy. To find out how the kitchen performs without him, Gordon instructs the owner and head chef to have dinner in the restaurant together, to work out their differences, and tells them that he will take care of the kitchen. However, what they do not know is that Gordon actually makes the other chefs run the kitchen in turn, to see how the kitchen runs without the head chef, and to see what the sous-chefs are made of and how they perform under pressure. Gordon notices that the kitchen actually runs much better without the head chef, the food is better, and it is a much happier place. Unfortunately, Gordon is unable to convince the owner to replace the current head chef, even though the kitchen runs better without him. As Gordon explains, "it is not up to him to make this decision, this is up to the owner himself."

For any organization it is crucial to have the proper people, with the fitting attitude and appropriate skillset doing a job which they enjoy and where they excel in. This fit between the requirements of the job and capabilities of the person is fundamental. People who fit their job are more satisfied with their work, perform better, are committed and identify themselves with the organization they work for. And yet, so many restaurants have the wrong people in the kitchen, front of house, and leading the team.

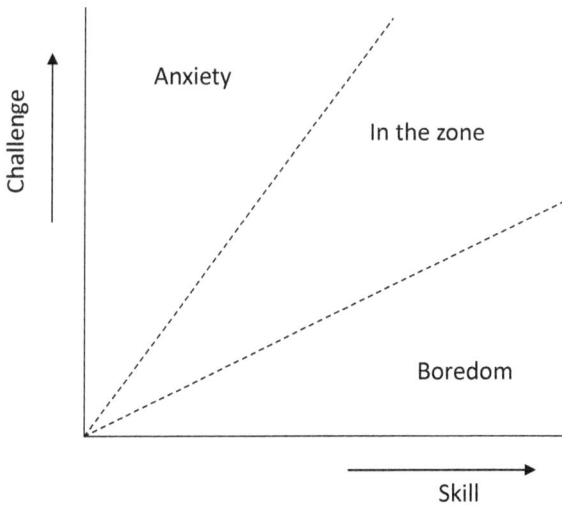

Figure 10: Need to match the level of challenge and skill

To align the right person with the right job one of the Gordon's key activities is to determine the level of cooking and front-of-house skills in the group. One of the techniques to discover the capabilities of current staff is to rotate staff in different positions. Gordon's brutal and provocative honesty is also very useful in this respect, because this teaches him who has the bullocks to actually tell the truth. Moreover his games are largely designed to spot talent. When talent is available Gordon can replace nonperforming individuals or he can decide to change the current configuration. The end goal of such a recombination of individuals is to create a winning, mutually supporting team from a group of nonperforming individuals whose capabilities are wasted in their current jobs. As Gordon comments, "Too many individuals ruin a business."

Obviously, the most important position in the restaurant is the owner. Unfortunately the owner cannot be changed that easily (although this might often be the proper thing to do). The next best option is often to find an appropriate task that suits the capabilities of the owner and contributes to the needs of the restaurant. If such a solution cannot be found, perhaps a function has to be invented for the owner, to minimize the amount of damage that they do to the restaurant. For example, owner Sandy does not really contribute to her restaurant, Morgan's. Gordon creates a new position for her (i.e., to sell antiques between dishes) just to keep her from meddling in. Another example is provided by The Fenwick Arms, where owner Brian, who has the memory span of a 2-year old due to a heart attack, creates complete chaos in the kitchen. Gordon has to try his ultimate best to keep him out of there and creates a position as the lead campaigner for the campaign for real gravy. In The Walnut Tree

Inn, Gordon even goes so far as to draw a line on the kitchen floor that prevents owner Francesco from entering the kitchen and interfering with the cooking.

First class people hire first class people; second class people hire third class people

Manfred Kets de Vries

For the chef and the rest of the staff of a restaurant, more options exist. For example, people that are not adding value can simply be fired, like in the case of Momma Cherry's, where Gordon instructs Charita to fire those who are not adding any value to prevent the restaurant from impending doom. In Piccolo Teatro, incompetent and arrogant head chef Daniel is also fired, to make way for young Indie, who is more than capable and eager to learn. Many more examples can be found where people are fired to make way for more competent people.

The great importance of having the right people on board is also confirmed in other business studies. According to Jim Collins most CEO's immediately start by setting a new direction or by articulating a fresh corporate vision. This is completely wrong. Leaders of successful companies do not start with "where to go" but with "who to bring along." They start by getting the right people on board, the wrong people off, and the right people in the right seats. First you put the right people in the right place, the right direction will then swiftly follow.

The alternative is to point the direction, but then you risk losing the support of the organization and its major stakeholders. This happened effectively to Kermit Campbell. He was named chairman of Herman Miller (a $1billion furniture company). In the same year the company recorded its first ever loss. Kermit Campbell quickly moved to cut costs by firing several top execs as well as closing plants and showrooms. The caused tremendous resistance to change but Campbell was not impressed; "Survival is more important than maintaining a pristine relationship with workers." Although this may be the case, the end result was that Mr. Campbell was forced to announce his retirement only two months after taking the job.

VI. FREEZE

In medicine, a distinction is made between the mind (i.e., the psychological plane) and the body (i.e., the physical plane). While a doctor can cure the physical (body) disease of a patient through medicine and surgery, the mental disease (mind) is often much more difficult to cure. We probably all know someone who has suffered from a stroke due to an unhealthy lifestyle (e.g., smoking, alcohol, and junk food), only to continue with the same pattern after being released from the hospital. The reason is that we are creatures of habit, and these habits are extremely difficult to change. In a way, these habits have imprinted certain patterns (i.e., by creating neurological connections) in our minds, and deviating from these patterns causes discomfort and anxiety.

To change our habits, prolonged repetition of new habits is often needed to effectively imprint a different pattern that effectively 'overrules' or cancels out our old dysfunctional pattern. This is not easy, and requires continues effort on our part, as it is extremely easy to digress and revert back to old habits and patterns, especially in stressful situations. Unfortunately, the only thing that a doctor can do is have the patient revisit him at certain intervals, to make sure that the patient behaviour follows doctors' advice.

The same logic applies to organizational rescue. While it is relatively easy to implement physical changes (e.g., implementing new routines, procedures, governance, and structures), changing the culture of the organization is much more difficult. However, it is the culture of the organization that time and again determines whether changes are lasting or whether the organization reverts back to its old ways. Changing the behaviour is relatively easy when the turnaround manager is involved and can observe the organization members, and to correct any dysfunctional behaviour. But what will happen when the turnaround manager leaves? The answer to this question lies completely in the hands of management, as it depends on their willingness and ability to correct any dysfunctional behaviour. The fact that they have been responsible for the failure in the first place does not really speak to their advantage. What is needed are ways to institutionalize the changes in the organization, to make them part of the culture and the organization's normal operations. In the words of Kurt Lewin (1947): "A change towards a higher level of group performance is frequently short-lived, after a 'shot in the arm', group life soon returns to the previous level. This indicates that it does not suffice to define the objective of planned change in group performance as the reaching of a different level. Permanency of the new level, or permanency for a desired period, should be included in the objective."

While the chances of a relapse are diminished in the case of successful change, there is no guarantee whatsoever that owners and staff will not return to their old habits and behaviours. Despite the success that the turnaround provides, it is part of human nature to return to old habits and behaviours. For this reason, on many occasions do we witness restaurateurs going back to old menus, bringing back elements of the old interior decoration, and regressing to their old routines and behaviour. To install lasting changes, it is imperative try and prevent this from happening.

To avoid the organization and its members from regressing into dysfunctional behaviour, a set of techniques is needed to validate the changes. In this chapter, we will discuss a number of the techniques that can lead to more lasting changes.

Change Principle 26: Appoint Guards

In The Fenwick Arms Gordon confides with Elaine. Gordon has removed owner Brian from the kitchen. Brian cannot cook properly anymore after his heart surgery. Before the turnaround his kitchen was a disaster zone and his food ridiculous. Luckily, the turnaround has been a great success; the new chef creates better food and the restaurant is visibly improving, attracting new and happy customers. But there is a problem on the horizon. Brian wants to go back to being the chef. He misses his old job. He feels unfit after losing his identity as a cook. Gordon senses Brian's unhappiness. Before he leaves The Fenwick Arms, he appoints Elaine, Brain's wife, as a guard. He says that she should avoid Brian's return to the kitchen at all costs. This will not be good for Brian's health and it will be a disaster for the restaurant.

Appointing protectors of the change so that the organization does not return to the old situation is important in the last phase of the turnaround. When a turnaround manager leaves the organization, the organization has the natural tendency to revert back to the old equilibrium. Appointing people who have an explicit role in order to prevent a return to the old, dismal, situation is a way to secure the sustainability of the change.

But appointing guards does not guarantee sustainability. For one thing, being a guard is a tough job. Guards must be strong enough to hold the old forces at bay. In many cases guards are not strong enough. When Gordon has turned the Piccolo Teatro, the vegetarian restaurant in Paris, into a restaurant with sexy vegetarian food, he is not convinced of the sustainability of the change. Although owner Rachel says she is committed to the change, she is in fact lazy and clumsy. Gordon therefore asks the help of Rachel's father (and financier) to keep his daughter on the right track. Gordon also gives advice to Indie, the new and talented chef, to keep going and drive the restaurant. However, appointing these two guards has little impact as owner Rachel who does not listen to the advice of her father or her young chef. She remains irresponsible and selfish. This quickly leads to the closure of the restaurant. In Gordon words: "restaurants close easily, especially when the owner is not 100% committed."

There are very few people who possess the strength, power, and mandate to override an owner and become an effective guard. Family members and sometimes a critical resource (e.g. chef) are often the only persons who have any influence. But even then the job of a guard is almost impossible. In The Runaway Girl, the girlfriend of owner Justin is pretty clear about this: "he does not listen to me."

You can't teach an old dog new tricks

Old English Saying

In the world of addictions, relapse prevention (RP) is an important field of study aimed at identifying and preventing situations where there is a high-risk of the former addict returning to his or her old ways. There are several ways to cope with this so-called relapse risk. For example, former addicts are often asked to create a list with warning signs and combine these warning signs with possible actions to use in these risky situations. Another well-known strategy is to create a support network of people around you who support the change and prevent you from slipping back into your old ways;; they act as your guards. These persons are aware of their role as guard, supporter of change and are always available on speed dial.

Lululemon Athletica is a yoga-inspired athletic apparel company with a chain of international clothing stores. The company was founded by Dennis Wilson in 1998 based on his firm belief in yoga as the best technique to sustain physical fitness. Currently, the firm has over 201 stores and plans to grow significantly in the coming years. At the same time, Lululemon is very concerned about maintaining the unique culture and values of the company; i.e. how to keep its cult? The answer of Luluman is to establish a strong culture with clear guidelines and a role for culture bearers. For instance, the organization talks a lot about being egoless, so that feedback can be "real." Being egoless is an aspiration that is talked about and modelled every day while guarded and upheld by employees, clients and local yogis who act as Luluman's ambassadors.

Change Principle 27: Create Symbols of Successful Change

La Parra de Burriana, the restaurant on the Spanish coast, has lost the support of the local community by making a mess out of the annual dinner of the Donkey Sanctuary, a local charity. For Gordon, this is a deadly sin as it destroys the restaurants reputation within the local community; a lifeline in winter in all holiday resorts. After the successful turnaround Gordon leaves the Spanish coast and La Parra de Burriana. But before Gordon disappears, he leaves a small statue of a Donkey behind. He places this donkey strategically in the front of the restaurant so that owner Lawrence will never forget that he always has to take care of the local community. It is a strong reminder of failures in the past to prevent future relapses.

In La Lanterna, the restaurant owned by "A1 6HEF" Alex, Gordon leaves behind a menu which says (in small print): "no use of microwave, all fresh ingredients." This aims to prevent the return of Alex to his old ways (he has the habit of putting frozen industrial prepared meals in the microwave). In Campania, the New Jersey restaurant, Gordon ends the turnaround by smashing all the big plates. These plates are a symbol of the old ways of Campania; tremendous waste through enormous portions and an outsized inventory. The smashing of plates provides owner Joe, his wife Melissa and the rest of the staff with a powerful reminder of the old ways and to prevent regression.

A charming example of symbolism can be found in the Fish and Anchor where ex-boxer Mike got his recipes out of cookbooks written by famous chefs. At the beginning of this episode, Mike was forced to get rid of all his cookbooks. But when Gordon leaves the Fish and Anchor he gives Mike an empty cookbook to put his own recipes in writing. The empty exercise book is a powerful reminder of what Gordon in essence has tried to teach Mike: you have to be your own man.

In some cases Gordon leaves behind more than just a symbol. For instance in fine dining restaurant La Riviera Gordon introduces the 'chefs table'; a dining table placed in the kitchen. "Such a table keeps the chef on his toes and increases his focus on the customer." This is important as conceited chef Loic has a tendency not to be bothered by customers. The introduction of the 'chefs table' creates a much stronger link between chef and customer ensures better and faster feedback. It is a constant reminder and symbol of the importance of the customer.

A last example of a potent reminder of the new identity is a new annual marketed event such as French Anglo Oyster competition that Gordon fabricates in the episode on The Sandgate Hotel. This is a powerful reminder of the newfound Anglo-French identity of the restaurant. The idea is that in starting an annual event which is well followed by the local press, the Anglo-French character will become part of The Sandgate Hotel's heritage and thus it becomes much harder to slip back into the old ways.

It is hard to overestimate the importance of symbols. Symbols are a formidable form of communication that is even more fundamental than conscious cognition. There is so much information lying in symbols and objects. Often long before a person talks to someone, one gathers (largely unconsciously) enormous amounts of information about the other person based on what they wearing and how they behave. These symbols can reveal important information (or misinformation) about one's mood, occupation, personality, opinions, class, and even sexual desires. The power of symbols is well understood by organizations. It is the primary reason why medical advertisements often parade a "doctor" in a white coat. The marketing department knows that the white coat is a powerful symbol which helps to persuade viewers of the trustworthiness of the promoted drug. Life is a set of symbols. When properly used, we can change people and businesses through the power of symbols.

Symbols can come in all sort of guises. Stories can be as powerful as visible symbols. For instance, the culture of Apple was enforced by the stories about Steve Jobs firing people on the spot if he did not like a design. These vivid stories enforced the culture that Apple employees must pay attention to detail and that user experience is crucial. Through these stories all employees understood that if you don't pay attention to detail, you will be fired.

Change Principle 28: Validate the Change

Nothing is more convincing than success. Michel, the stubborn owner of The Secret Garden is not convinced of the changes Gordon suggests. All the proposed modifications are resisted by Michel, from early adjustments in the décor ("I do not like it") to the new menu ("your new menu is not better than mine"). But Gordon nevertheless forces these changes trough. Luckily, the customers seem to love the new décor and the new menu. Michel is suspicious, so he decides to ask the customers personally to see what they think of the new menu and the new décor. With each enthusiastic evaluation Michel becomes more upset. But eventually the quarter drops; the customers are happy and there is over 3,000 dollars (60 customers spending $50 each) in the cash register. Confronted with all the evidence, Michel is won over and he admits that he has been in the wrong all along.

The above does not depict the ideal way of operating. Gordon, as any turnaround manager, would rather have the full support of the owners regarding suggested changes. Sadly, in many cases this is a bridge too far as most owners are in deep denial. But what is often possible in a turnaround is to get permission to make a small change. This is what Gordon does. He seeks permission to change at least one dish on the menu. This is almost always a special. Then he makes sure that this special is a success and customers are really enthusiastic about it and that the special is a true money spinner. This success then validates further change.

A good example is Campania, the Italian restaurant in New Jersey. After cooking with the kitchen staff, Gordon suggests that Campania needs a signature dish and he proposes meatballs. When Gordon describes a great recipe for meatballs to the kitchen staff, they are thrilled. Straight away Gordon takes the chefs to the local market and has them give away free samples with funny t-shirts which says; *"New Jersey's Best Meatballs."* Everybody has a good time and, more importantly, the customers really enjoy the food. In the evening the meatballs have a prominent space on the old menu and the customers love it. Because of the great reactions, the proposed changes are immediately validated. Basically the same approach can be found in The Secret Garden, Trobiano's, La Gondola where the specials are all getting immediate enthusiastic reviews, thereby enabling Gordon to take the next step of the turnaround.

In a couple of cases the introduction of the special is completely rejected. For instance, in The Walnutt Tree Inn Gordon wants to show Francisco that the new proposed dish with scallops is as nice as the previous dish, but costs four pounds less thus making a profit. Unfortunately, Francisco is not interested, and bluntly says that the new dish with a scallop less does not fit his type of restaurant. He would not even try it as a special. Gordon: "You are so stubborn. It is like talking to a freeze block. I'll go home, you continue struggling."

The function of introducing a specialty dish in the above examples is comparable to the function of quick-wins in many organizational changes. The change is often small enough to persuade managers and staff to agree with it, sometimes even support it, and the realization that the quick-win is a strong persuader of doubters of the organizational change. Jack Welch, the former CEO of GE called this 'change fast'.

Change Principle 29: Revisit Regularly

When Gordon revisited The Priory, the 100-seater restaurant in Sussex, England owned by former IT consultant Scott, he finds the place in shambles. Six weeks after the turnaround, the restaurant has slipped from 800 coverts to 300 coverts. Gordon: "I am infuriated with Scott, he is so weak willed and forgotten the lesson of marketing. You are a salesman? Then drive it." Instead of leaving, Gordon stays and shows commitment to the turnaround. He shocks Scott into action, says that he has to remove his tie and put on his marketing smile. Gordon takes Scott and his team out on the streets. Within 30 minutes the Priory is fully booked. Gordon: "You have to drive it, and do not stop driving it. Business does not come and sit on your lap, you have to look for it and find it."

Gordon also revisits Silversmiths (formerly known as The Runaway Girl) in Sheffield, England just three months after the worldwide credit crunch in 2008. Given the economic situation it is no wonder that both restaurants are not doing very well. In Silversmiths the sales skyrocketed at first, but after the credit crunch they are barely making any money. Gordon: "it is not about making money, but about survival." For Silversmiths Gordon invents pie-night. Pies are cheap to make and this may attract customers during the week who are looking for a cheap but fresh meal. Gordon is also starting a campaign to support local restaurants and tries to lure away customers from the chain restaurants to Silversmiths by handing out flyers in these establishments.

The above examples demonstrate that one of the most powerful instruments to prevent a relapse to the old situation is a revisit. On the one hand a revisit of Gordon will prevent people slipping back into their old ways, on the other hand, this enables Gordon to correct any failures made during the time between the turnaround and revisit. There are typically six weeks to three months between the turnaround and Gordon's revisit. The revisit can also help by giving extra confidence and energy to the change effort. In The Sandgate Hotel, Gordon brings a sea bass for the chef as a challenge to cook for Gordon. This reinforces the identity of the restaurant (fresh fish), but also demonstrates Gordon's faith in the chef.

Just like a doctor who keeps a regular check-up to see if all is well, a turnaround manager should visit sometimes and see whether all is progressing according to plan. Just like health check-ups, a revisit of the turnaround manager can help to pinpoint problems before they mature, improving the chance for remedy and cure.

Change Principle 30: Give Fatherly Advice

Gordon typically ends the show with some fatherly advice to the owner and chef; a powerful reminder of all the difficulties that have to be overcome. So in Clubway 41 Gordon reminds Nigel that a restaurant does not have to be the best. "You just have to be a little bit better than the rest" and "You are only as good as your last service." To Lois, the faint-hearted owner of The Sandgate Hotel, he says: "Do not fall in love with it, it is a job."

Gordon's departure is not always friendly. To Steve, the chef of La Gondola: "I'll be back, if you will be here when I come back is another matter." Gordon was right in this case as Steve left four months later to start working in a pub. To Sebastian, the owner of the Californian pizzeria with the same name, he says: "The menu changed, the staff has changed…but there is one thing that has not changed…and that is you Sebastian."

Gordon then continues: "I never, never, ever, ever, ever, met someone I believe in as little as you. I think that you will go back to your sloppy, short cut, five out of ten, frozen ways. Good luck!" Gordon then slaps Sebastian on the back and disappears. He uses the departure as his last possibility to influence someone. To Alex, the chef and owner of La Lanterna, he says: "I think you will not make it...and I tell you now in order to prove me wrong." But at the same time he also gives Alex more fatherly advice: "Do not try to run before you can walk."

In the case of Paul Bazzini, the chef/owner of Bazzini's Gordon tells Paul that he has not changed enough to turn this restaurant around. Paul simply needs to accept the hard truth that he has not got the makings of a leader. Paul disagrees and says that he is a leader. Gordon: "You always say the right things, but you have to do the right things. Good luck."

In some episodes Gordon leaves behind more than friendly advice. Especially in the American episodes he sometimes arranges the help of a trusted advisor. This person will help and guide the turnaround in the weeks and months after Gordon's departure. For instance, in Dillon's Gordon calls in the help of Vikash as a consulting Indian chef, and in Lido di Manhattan Beach he requires the assistance of Scotty who rescues the restaurant when Luis and Arturo leave and who will provide a proper example for a month after Gordon leaves. In Hot Potato Café, Gordon calls in the help of Richard Marsh as a mentor for the young, inexperienced, but talented chef Danielle.

VII. CONCLUSIONS

Organizational development and change (and organization science more broadly) brings together many disciplines from the social sciences, such as, psychology, management, sociology, behavioural science, motivation, and learning. However, as we have argued at the beginning that due to a fragmentation between these scientific domains, there is a mismatch between the theory and practice of organizational development and change. In this book, we have set out to close this gap between theory and practice, by adopting a threefold strategy. First, we have employed the paradigm of grounded theory to build our arguments from what we observed in practice, instead of using observation to prove preconceived notions about organizational change and development. Second, we have used objective data that is publicly available, so that any bias due to the subjective interpretations of the data becomes apparent to the reader. Third, we did utilize a medical analogy to further distance ourselves from our preconceived notions on organizational development and change. This novel approach has led to many insights and understandings that bring theory and practice closer together. These new insights are described in the first section of this final chapter; what should we learn from reality TV-stars.

As has become clear from our comparison of the state of medical science with the state of organization science (which contains organizational change and development), organization science is just a new kid on the block and still has a long way to go before it even approaches the state of medical science.[8] In our opinion, what is needed in the study of organizational change is a better understanding of the anatomy of healthy organizations combined with a deeper insight into the pathology of organizational failure; how does organizational failure starts and how does it progress? In this book we aim to share some basic insights of autonomy and pathology. In the first chapter, we have already described the anatomy of healthy organizations in ten different qualities or X-factors. In the second section of this seventh chapter we describe the pathology of organizational failure. In both cases we can only provide the reader with a rough sketch. In medicine, many scholars have contributed to our current understanding of the human body, the intricate interdependencies between the systems of which it is composed, and the development of different pathologies. Additionally, we realize that our sample is not representative for the whole organizational population as we have only studied relatively small restaurants. As such, we think that these pathologies of change that we deducted from the TV-shows are most appropriate for like

---

[8] We have to note, however, that medical science is a natural science, while organization science is a social science. Natural sciences are generally referred to as 'hard' sciences, while social sciences are considered 'soft', where hard means being more scientific, rigorous, or accurate. In laymen's terms, harder sciences can make much stronger and basic predictions, as there is a greater possibility to conduct controlled experiments.

organizations, i.e., small and medium sized enterprises. Therefore this final chapter ends with a brief discussion of the books implications for organizational change in large multi-national organizations instead of small and medium sized firms.

What can we learn from reality-TV?

What can be learned from this book? After all, a lot of the techniques which are described in this book are well known in the psychology and management literature. For example, anyone who has ever studied organizational change knows about the importance of quick wins and a clear vision, and anyone who knows anything about psychology will tell you about the importance of building rapport and the causes of resistance. Furthermore, many of the principles in this book have been described extensively in the literature, and even the structure of the book is based on two existing theories of change (i.e., Lewin's three stage model and control theory). So, a big part of this book should not be new to academics. However, several of the principles described in this book are new and have, as far as we know, not been properly identified in the literature. Moreover, there are also a number of findings that actually are at odds with current knowledge.

Therefore we will describe 15 principles of turnaround success that are currently not or not fully part of the (academic) literature. These 15 amendments are:

- Treat the cause, not the symptoms (it starts from the top)

Many books on organizational change advise to start with the so-called low hanging fruit and generate quick wins to increase the commitment to change and prevent resistance from taking hold. For example, by creating a special dish that is easy to prepare and will result in instant success. It is often argued that nothing motivates more than success, and in this way, a turnaround manager can validate his ability to lead the organization into a better future. Although quick wins definitely serve a purpose, they should never compromise the priority of the larger issue at hand. This means that quick wins should only be used to complement the main task of combating the main problem(s) facing the organization. What is needed first is a clear and visible act to combat the underlying cause of failure, to demonstrate the sincerity of the change effort, and the willingness to attack the root cause. Otherwise, you run the risk of increasing resistance, as staff might start to doubt the true intentions of the change effort and reduce their commitment to the change project. For example, if the main problem of a failing restaurant is an arrogant chef and reluctant owner, then introducing a new dish without dealing with the main cause tends to become counterproductive. If the change project is not visibly tackling the main issues (i.e., the arrogant chef and reluctant owner), staff will – more often than not – retreat from the change project and lower their commit to change. We believe that in many organizations, this is exactly what happens. Instead of dealing with a failing CEO and board of directors (these are ultimately responsible for the performance of the organization), a new product is introduced and staff is asked to put an extra effort (e.g., lower wages, extra hours, et cetera) to put the organization back on track.

- Organizational failure is always individual failure

Although many books on organizational failure point to the importance of leadership and key individuals, there is often no clear connection between organizational and individual failure. However, as we argue in this book, organizational failure always implies individual failure and the root cause of organizational and individual failure always lies in individual denial. This implies that the cause of organizational failure is always rooted in individual psychology, and any organizational change project should thus pay explicit attention to the psychology of key individuals. The role of individual psychology is often downplayed, and one assumes that task and responsibilities can simply be reassigned, as if individuals are perfectly substitutable entities with like capabilities. To put the organization back on track and restore profitability, it is simply believed that all that is needed is a new organizational chart, without proper attention to how individual failure was created in the first place or how it was allowed to persist over time. Organizational performance is dependent upon individual performance, and increasing organizational performance requires structuring the organization in such a way as to maximize the performance of individuals. While it is certainly possible that non-performance of certain key individuals can lead to organizational failure, and replacing this individual with another is part of the solution, one should always ask oneself what made failure possible in the first place. Knowledge about what caused the failure and its persistence is extremely helpful in preventing the failure to happen in the future and, if it does, to detect it as soon as possible.

- Let them talk, but do not believe a word they say

As organizational change always implies individual change, and individual change is generally uncomfortable, there is often a great deal of resistance to change. Cognitive dissonance is a discomfort produced by holding conflicting cognitions (i.e., ideas, beliefs, values, and emotional reactions) simultaneously. To reduce this discomfort people make up excuses to keep their world of dreams intact and prevent any unwanted change to their cognition. Although the individual who uses a sophism (i.e., a seeming well-reasoned argument that is actually false) may actually believe it is true, these arguments are mere figments of their imagination. For this reason, it is important to trust no-one, and judge people on the basis of their actions instead of their words, in accordance with the saying, "actions speak louder than words." However, this does not mean that you can ignore whatever is being said. Quite the opposite, it is important to register what they are saying, as this provides important clues as to their 'sanity'. After all, the extent to which their words actually match their behaviours indicates the degree to which they have an accurate perception of reality and are free from denial. Hence, it is important to let them talk, but to initially doubt everything that is being said.

- Involve the social context

People do not exist in a vacuum, but are socially embedded. In the words of Robert Penn Warren (1946) in his Pulitzer Prize winning book "All the King's Men," "They say you are not you except in terms of relation to other people. If there weren't any other people there wouldn't be any you because what you do which is what you are, only has meaning in relation to other people." Paying attention to the individual psychology is important in a change project, but one should also realize that an individual's psychology is socially embedded, not only professionally in the organization, but also personally in relation with friends and family. An individual's psyche cannot be separated from this context, and the individual's psychology in the workplace must match their psychology at home. This means that changing an individual's psychology in the workplace has consequences for their personal environment as well. On the one hand, this is good news, as a changed and healthier work environment will result in a better personal environment. On the other hand, however, this also means that resistance to change might have its origin in the personal environment of the individual as well, which lies beyond the direct influence of the change/turnaround manager.

- Provocation is needed to uncover denial

Many change books lack guidance towards the behaviour of the turnaround manager, and the ones that do usually stress the importance of diplomacy to prevent upsetting staff or management. However, provocative behaviour is often needed to break through people's shell. To establish a sense of urgency, the turnaround manager has to break through the shield of denial in any way possible, and this can require confrontational and perhaps even insulting behaviour. Emotions are usually blocked by anger, and to connect to other emotions (e.g., passion for business, love for food, care for people) the anger first needs to be released. And to do this, you simply need a stick. Merely asking people to release their anger to connect to other emotions simply will not cut it. Some genuine tough love is needed here, and one needs to be pushed and poked to chase away the beast that stands in front of the cave of our emotions. It goes without saying that this is a challenging endeavour and a strategy that is not fit for all, as it takes courage to confront and provoke others, especially if they are the one that pay your salary. Going against the saying, "do not bite the hand that feeds you," is not completely without risk however, and can result in losing your job. However, sometimes it is necessary to get to the real cause of failure, and "drastic situations require drastic measures."

- Pressure is needed to reveal failure

Generally, there is not much real work to be done in a failing business, as orders and customers are largely absent. Of course, often staff is busy playing blame games, avoiding responsibilities, gossiping, and pointing fingers. However, pressure or challenge is needed to reveal weaknesses in the organization's processes, routines, and behaviours. While individuals might function as perfect little angels at fifty percent of their capacity, they might turn into complete monsters around ninety or a hundred percent of their capabilities, and start to verbally abuse colleagues, customers, and suppliers. Obviously, this interferes with the smooth functioning of the organization, and needs to be prevented at all costs. Therefore, what is needed is to push individuals and the organization to its limits, to find the weakest link in the chain, and determine what needs to be improved to prevent a future melt down. So, in the same way as a doctor increases the stress on the human body to reveal any abnormalities, stress can also be increased in different parts of the organization (and/or selected individuals) to make the organizational abnormalities apparent. This way, these abnormal variations can be dealt with to prevent them revealing themselves in the heat of the battle, such as, when the organization is trying to fill certain orders for important clients that influence its future prosperity (e.g., consider the case of a melt-down of the chef during a visit of an important food critic).

- Connect smartly to get your message across

Nowadays, connected leadership is a buzzword, but this is exactly what is needed in a challenging turnaround situation. We have already mentioned on several occasions that organizational change implies individual change, which brings the discomfort associated with cognitive dissonance, that can turn into resistance to change. People in denial have built a wall around themselves that prevents any message that does not conform to their belief system to enter their awareness. What happens is that a simple label is attached to the sender that invalidates the contents of the message. To see how this process works, consider receiving a message or advice that is rather confronting (e.g., the way you have been doing this or that for past ten years is wrong) from someone that you perceive to be envious of you, insane, malicious, or merely looking for trouble to increase entertainment value (like in the case of a TV-show such as Kitchen Nightmares). How would you respond? To make sure that your messages do not get invalidated in this way, it is important to really connect, so that the message is received in the right way and has the opportunity to sink in. Connectedness is accomplished not only through words but also through behaviour (remember, actions speak louder than words). The best way that this can be accomplished depends on the specific setting and context, and the opportunities that this presents. For example, in Kitchen Nightmares, Gordon often helps with cleaning the kitchen, which is always well received by staff and owners. This tells them that he is serious, and genuinely concerned with the restaurant. It also creates an opportunity to engage in a good conversation with staff members and to connect with them. Sometimes it means really getting your hands dirty, at others you have to open up first (e.g., in many episodes Gordon tries to connect to people by opening up, and sharing personal information first), and on occasion it is enough to spend some time together. What is needed is a feeling of a real connection, so that they can open up to you, and be honest about their concerns, doubts, and challenges. This way, you really understand their behaviour, and are in a much better position to advise and propose changes, as they fit much better with the psychology of the individual and are usually well received.

Obviously, it is not always wise to try to connect with others, and this strategy should be used wisely. Sometimes the situation might require you to disconnect even further, and to completely disengage, or even to walk away. Basically, you should use any means that leads to a real connection, where information is shared honestly, without hidden agendas and ulterior motives. This is an interesting and telling feature within existing organizational change practices. For instance Stuart M. Klein (1996) states that the strategy in the initial phase of an organizational change should be aimed to reassure managers and employees. This is in fact totally the opposite of what we believe is needed in a turnaround situation. It does not help to reassure people and to restore confidence, as they already have too much of both. It is better to undermine it, to destabilize the self-assurance of individuals and groups, and shake the little comfortable (dream-)world that they have built for themselves, and follow the advice of Kurt Lewin (1947: 229), "To break open the shell of complacency and self-righteousness it is sometimes necessary to bring about an emotional stir up."

- Games and metaphors are needed to overcome resistance

Due to denial, cognitive dissociation, and resistance, direct communication about certain aspects can be too confronting for some organizational members. They simply raise their defenses and disqualify all messages or attempts at real communication. In this instance, it often helps to take the issue out of its context using games and metaphors. The emotional response is tied to the context, and not to the issue itself. While being perfectly logical and rational, a certain point or argument is simply invalidated because it threatens an individual's well-being. Taking the individual out of the equation through games and metaphors enables you. When they fully agree with you in this safe and non-threatening situation, and the message has truly sunken in, you can simply ask them to apply the same point or message to their own situation. This way, they can connect the dots themselves, and it is not you who is criticizing them, but they actually criticize themselves. And then cannot invalidate their own messages and critique. Hence, games and metaphors are a perfect way to get painful and confronting messages across without being the messenger. Despite the well-known advice of "don't shoot the messenger," this more often happens than not, and it is better to have the individual be their own messenger.

- Fun and humour are needed to release tension

Ensure that there is loads of time for fun and enjoyment in a change process. This is crucial as turning a place around will cost tremendous amounts of energy of all involved. This is even more important as the owner and members of staff are already low on spirit before the turnaround has to start. Having to cook and serve for a near empty restaurant day in, day out and losing lots of money in this process has often drained everybody's energy even before the turnaround begins. There are three reasons why a turnaround is such an energy absorber. First, there is the denial, resistance, and confrontation. This naturally costs a lot of energy as we all know. Second, there is the acceptance of failure. To finally accept that have been making mistakes also costs energy. Third, even if the failure is accepted and you are enthusiastically working on a new and improved solution (e.g., restaurant, menu, dish, and ambiance), this still is quite intensive as it takes a lot of extra work to turn a restaurant around. The enormous energy consumption in all phases of the turnaround implies that the effort should be structured in such a way that plenty of new vigor is provided for. One of the best ways to provide energy is to laugh and do fun things together. You need to combine fun and humour with important turnaround activities in order to sustain an organizational change.

- Use many means of communication to get your message across

In communication theory, a distinction is made between the sender, receiver, and the message itself. Often the intention of the sender is taken as being most important in describing the meaning of the message. The problem with this definition is, however, that the intention often remains buried, for several reasons. For example, the sender might not be very proficient in transcribing his intentions into a message that can be clearly understood by others, or perhaps the receiver is not capable of translating the message back into the sender's intent (e.g., if the receiver is in denial). Defining the message on the basis of the sender's intent places the responsibility of interpreting the message in the right way at the receiving end in the communication. In our opinion, much can be gained if the responsibility of the message is placed with the sender. After all, as it is his intent to get a certain message across, it should also be his responsibility that the message is properly understood (i.e., interpreted correctly by the receiver). If the receiver of the message denies the message, another approach is required to make sure that the message sinks in and is understood correctly. This may imply that you need to find someone else to give the message, for example, customers, staff members, partners, or experts. If this does not cut it, yet another approach is required, perhaps by confronting them with objective facts or by provoking them to break through their denial. Yet another approach is to use games and metaphors, as these strip away the (uncomfortable) emotions that trigger denial.

If a message does not come through, you should not alter the message, but also look for alternative means to get the message across. As a rule, communication that provides an actual experience is much stronger than some words on a piece of paper. So do not give hope easily and be creative in finding your means of communication, and look for the response to the communication to determine whether the message has sunken in.

* Strike while the iron is hot

This old proverb clearly alludes to the imagery of the blacksmith, who works with metals such as iron, shaping them into a useful or decorative manner. If he delays in shaping the iron when it is hot, the metal soon cools and hardens and the opportunity is lost. This saying also applies in the turnaround process. On many occasions, an opportunity to implement change presents itself. This opportunity needs to be seized immediately, otherwise the iron cools down and the opportunity is lost. People are emotional creatures, and organizational turnarounds are an emotional undertaking. The characteristics of emotions are that they are highly fleeting. What feels good in this moment might not feel so good the next moment, and the perfect solution today might be considered the biggest mistake tomorrow. Therefore, if the right opportunity presents itself, seize it with both arms before it disappears. Often times, inaction or analysis paralysis (i.e., overanalyzing a situation, so that a decision or action is never taken, in effect paralyzing the outcome) has steered the organization towards failure. Especially, if the organizational culture is one of blame games and finger pointing, this strategy is high on the agenda of organizational members, and provides a dangerous trap for any turnaround manager. To prevent this kind of behaviour during the turnaround process, seize the opportunity when it presents itself by taking direct action.

- The turnaround manager should truly understand the industry

We have discussed this subject already in the former section. We think that a detailed understanding of the industry is crucial for four reasons. First, it makes harder for owner and staff to discredit the change manager. A turnaround stirs up emotions that often lead to resistance. To resist changes, organizational members start to make up excuses to prevent the need to change. One common strategy is to attack the turnaround manager and their skill set. Lacking intimate knowledge about the industry makes it difficult to effectively counter such attacks, and to prevent them from infecting the whole organization. Any counter argument (e.g., industry knowledge is not important, general process knowledge is) can be interpreted by them as an mere attempt to reveal the fact that you lack industry knowledge, and is thus not particularly effective in diffusing this threat. The second reasons why deep industry knowledge is important is that it enables the turnaround manager to distinguish between valid arguments and sophisms. For example, statements like "this is how we do things in the business" are much easier to invalidate with intimate knowledge about the business. Third, it enables the change/turnaround manager to assess the situation, and do this swiftly. Especially when there is a tight schedule, this can be very important. After all, because no one can be trusted at first sight, the change manager does need to form their own opinion, and knowledge about the business makes this process much more expedient. Fourth, it helps the change manager to come up with suggestions (e.g. a new product introduction) that can change the cash-flow situation rapidly, and prevent the organization from going belly up.

- Always be prepared to walk away

As a change manager you must make the people understand that the organization has a gigantic problem when you leave and that you are their only hope for survival. By constantly reminding them that you will walk away if they do not listen to you, you will make them aware that there is a serious problem which they do not know how to tackle. They become aware of the elephant in the room. Compare this to Steve Jobs who, when he returned to Apple to save it, obtained the title of i-CEO (interim CEO) just to remind the board and Apple's staff that he will walk away if they would not listen to him. Of course it helps if you have the reputation of Steve Jobs or Gordon Ramsay, but this trick can be used by other change managers as well.

- Establishing a sense of urgency is simply insufficient

In many books on change, e.g., Kotter (1996) or Kanter, Stein, and Jick (1992), the first step to realize change is to establish a sense of urgency. The sense of urgency is very clear in the restaurants starring in Kitchen Nightmares; without any exception these restaurants are on their way to go bust within months without a proper turnaround. Their chances of survival are slim. Despite this gigantic burning platform the restaurant owners are doing nothing. In each and every episode the restaurant owner resembles the proverbial 'rabbit in the headlights' drawn to the lure of the oncoming car. A sense of urgency is thus by no means enough to shock people into action. This inaction is caused by a number of reasons such as a lack of creativity and vision, denial, and other reasons which are discussed later in this book. A sense of urgency is perhaps a necessary condition for change but it is by no means sufficient.

- A simple model of change leads to chaotic processes

The structure of this book is based on a very straightforward and simple control model (Figure 7). An informed practitioner or academic may point to the fact that this model is too simplistic and mechanistic, because in real life organizational change is perceived as a highly complex and chaotic process. For example, Alexander Styhre (2002: 348) in his study of organizational change states, "Taken together the organizational change activities could never follow a linear model of organizational change […] Rather than assuming that reality is well ordered, structured and predictable as in the Cartesian-Newtonian conception, it may be seen as flows of energy and information." In our opinion Alexander Sthyre is right in his observation that organizational change is in practice a chaotic and complex process. But we argue that this complexity is exactly because the underlying model of organizational change is so straightforward. In many cases the model behaves well; resistance is low and management takes the correct decisions. This will gradually lead to an organization that gradually performs on a higher plane. But with other parameters, this simple dynamic control model has the tendency to jump out of control.

From system theory we can deduct that for an organization to progress to a new and higher level of stability during a turnaround, four preconditions have to be place. First and foremost to achieve a new equilibrium and improve performance, it is crucial that **the turnaround manager is able to make the 'right' interventions**. The role of the turnaround manager can be likened to the slogan of the US Marine Corps, "Adapt, Improvise, and Overcome." This too appears highly simplistic, but, as any Marine will tell you, its proper application is in a life-and-death situation is extremely complex and takes many, many years of expert training. While turnaround management is not a literal life-and-death situation, it can be likened as such, as you are perceived by many as the enemy, who try to do anything to discredit you personally and invalidate your arguments. To make matters worse, you do not know who to trust, as anyone can be a double agent, and stab you in the back when you are not looking. As soon as a turnaround manager enters the organization, he must be fully aware and observe any signal, as these provide vital clues about the identity of the organizational member (i.e., friend or enemy). What is needed is a quick grasp on the problem at hand, accompanied with direct and swift action to diffuse a potentially lethal situation. Sometimes it backfires, and the situation worsens and additional action is needed to prevent the problems from escalating beyond control. Furthermore, due to the interdependent nature, a solution in part of the organization can trigger a problem in another part, what is known in the literature as a cascade of change (Hannan, Polos, and Carroll, 2007). Basically, organizational change is a highly complex process consisting of feedback systems that are highly interdependent. Often, different kinds of changes run parallel to one another, and it is impossible to predict their interaction beforehand. This requires close monitoring and on-the-spot modifications and adaptations, and it takes a great deal of skill and art to implement changes that do not spin out of control.

The second precondition of stability are determined by **the initial conditions of the company**. Sometimes the initial situation is severe and beyond rescue. This can be because the business is already near bankruptcy and turning the situation around will take too much time, or it can be that the resistance to change is too difficult to handle. This resistance does determine the room to maneuver for a turnaround manager. The degree of resistance is dependent upon a variety of factors, such as the personality of the owner, the reputation of the turnaround manager, the nature of the proposed changes, et cetera. What is common is that the degree of resistance will change during the turnaround process. If everything runs smoothly, resistance could disappear altogether, but in many cases the resistance will not go away. In some cases, it can even transforms itself from covert resistance to open defiance. Basically, the intensity of resistance is dependent upon the effective application of the change techniques described in this book as well as the perceived success of earlier changes.

The third precondition for stability is **systematic and frequent testing** of various dimensions is needed to establish whether the change is still going the right way. If you do not test, you will never know whether you are moving to or moving away from that equilibrium. Finally, **fast feedback loops** are needed to continuously correct incongruities between the desired and actual situation to improve performance and prevent a return to the old ways of behaviour. If the feedback loops has delays, it takes more time to correct wrong behaviour.

While general step-by-step action plans advocated in popular management books do provide value, the danger is that it gives a reader the impression of organizational change as being a highly rational and logical process that can be planned well in advance. In these books, it appears as if an organizational change project can be likened to the move to a new office building, a matter that can be solved by due consideration and proper planning. Things could not be further from the truth, as a turnaround is much more like Tuckman's (1965) storming phase; it is always somewhat chaotic, often controversial, by and large unpleasant, and sometimes even downright painful. In a turnaround a company is constantly in a flux where analysis, change, resistance, and feedback go hand in hand.

A First on Organizational Pathology

In medicine, the objective is to restore heath to sick patients, by curing the disease and restoring the patient's normal condition. To effectively do so, besides an intimate understanding of the human anatomy, the doctor also needs intimate knowledge about the different kinds of diseases that might have inflicted the patient. The study of disease is called pathology[9]. According to Crowley (2013) pathology studies the following four aspects of disease, which are: (1) its cause or etiology, (2) the mechanisms of development or pathogenesis, (3) the structural alterations of cells or morphological changes, and (4) the consequences or clinical manifestations. Insight into these aspects of a disease facilitates correct diagnosis and subsequent treatment of the disease. Perceiving organizational failure as a disease means developing the pathology

---

[9] The word pathology is from Ancient Greek πάθος, pathos, "feeling, suffering"; and -λογία, -logia, "the study of" (Wikipedia, 2012)

of organizational failure, which can be defined as follows: (1) cause/etiology – what was the cause of the failure in the first place?, (2) mechanisms of development – how has the initial cause led to organizational failure or substandard performance?, (3) structural alterations of organizational parts – how are the parts and processes of a failing organization structurally different from a non-failing organization?, and (4) the consequences of change – what are the consequences of organizational failure or what is likely to happen over time if failure persists? Next, we will describe each of these aspects in more detail, on the basis of the knowledge that we have gained so far.

Cause of disease (i.e., organizational failure)

The initial cause of the failure can have many origins. As mentioned previously, the most frequent causes are starting the business for the wrong reasons and poor management. Other examples are a poor choice of location, faulty expectations, a general lack of the following; strategy, planning, capital, skills, authenticity combined with poor communication and operational standards (Parsa et al., 2005; Schaeffer, 2011). As becomes clear from this brief list of possible causes, the origins of failure are diverse. This means that we have to dig deeper to reveal the common thread that binds it all together.

Failure implies that there is an error in the functioning of the organization, which implies a mismatch between the organization's actual and desired behaviour. While the origins of this mismatch can be numerous (e.g., changes in the environment, technology, or personnel), the responsibility for any long-lasting mismatch between desired and actual behaviour eventually lies with the owner (or management, in larger organizations). If he or she is aware of such a mismatch, it is his or her task to correct it, and to put the organization back on track. However, if the mismatch (i.e., the error in the organization's behaviour) is not corrected, this implies that it is either not detected or not properly corrected. This means that the image (i.e., perception) that the owner (management) has of the organization and its behaviour does not conform to reality (otherwise, the error would be detected and/or corrected in the proper way). Hence, if we assume that the owner (i.e., management) is not consciously steering towards failure of the restaurant, the common denominator that can be identified in all these causes is a false perception of the organization and its behaviour. In other words, the root cause of all failure is a false perception (or distortion) of reality of the owner (or management) of the organization. As long as they are not fully aware, they simply do not see the need, the importance, or the reason why they should change and take full responsibility. In other words, the individual simply does not understand the reason why change is necessary. After all, in their model of the world, there is simply nothing wrong with anything that they can change or are responsible for changing. Hence, unawareness of the reason to change in combination with the discomfort that change brings means resistance to change.

Unawareness + discomfort = resistance

Full awareness of the reasons why (i.e., full awareness of the fact, its consequence, and its responsibility) in combination with discomfort creates a willingness to face the challenge of change.

Awareness + discomfort = challenge

Thus, what is needed first is awareness, which implies that denial needs to be eradicated and overcome. Once denial is overcome, the individual opens up and learning and change can finally take place. To overcome denial, it is important to understand it fully, what causes it, and how it is embedded and maintained within the organization. Therefore, in this section, we will dissect denial even further.

The cause of this distorted view of reality lies in the process of denial, which comes in three basic forms, and is related to what is being denied. First, there is simple denial, which refers to the process where a fact is denied altogether, by distorting reality in such a way that the fact disappears. A nice example is Abby from Down City, who simply does not register the fact that the quality of food is below par. She distorts reality in such a way as to accommodate her belief that the quality of food is a "10 out of 10." Any signals that claim otherwise are simply registered by Abby as envy or insanity. The second form of denial is called minimization, and entails admitting the fact itself but denying its consequence (e.g., the seriousness of failure). This is actually a combination of denial and rationalization, commonly referred to as making excuses. Michel from the Secret Garden provides a perfect example, when he denies the importance of the mold-infections in the freezer that Gordon finds during his inspection of the kitchen. The third and last form of denial is called projection, where both the fact and its consequence are admitted, but the responsibility for the fact is denied.

The cause of this denial often lies in our infancy, when we instinctively use our senses and minds to make "sense" of the world. If we encounter a certain fact that is too painful or threatening to us, we simply deny its existence, its consequence, or responsibility. To further protect ourselves, we even deny these distortions (i.e., "I am not distorting reality"). Obviously, the cause of reality distortion does not need to lie in someone's childhood, and can also develop later in life. For example, consider the case where a restaurant is awarded a Michelin star because of the high quality and consistency of the served food. While this accomplishment is obviously a team effort, a common pattern that can be observed is that the head-chef attributes this success mostly to his skills and capabilities, and downplays the role of others. In an extreme form, the head-chef becomes arrogant and forms the belief that he knows exactly what customers want and is not interested in their opinion any more (e.g., consider head chef Loic from La Riviera). If we assume that the organizational members are physically healthy, in the sense that their sensory perceptions (i.e., sight, hearing, smell, taste, and feeling) are not impaired, this means that we can liken organizational failure to the existence of a mental disease in some of its organizational members. That is, if we define mental health as having an accurate representation of 'objective' reality, implying that there is no misperception of reality.

We have indicated that organizational failure always implies individual failure, and that the most important individual in the equation is the owner of the restaurant (i.e., the management of the organization). Other important individuals are the head-chef and the maître-d, as these are considered to be the managers of the kitchen and front of house, respectively. We do not deny that other individuals in the restaurant can also have an important influence on the functioning of the restaurant, especially in the case that the aforementioned not taking responsibility. However, for the sake of brevity and simplicity, we will focus on owner, head-chef, and maître-d.

Pathogenesis (i.e., the development of organizational failure)

Now that we know that the root cause of failure always lies in (the) denial (of reality), we can consider how this can lead to organizational failure. For this, we consider the basic evolutionary process that any business/organization undergoes. After all, it can occur at any stage of this process. In a highly simplified view, the basic stages of any restaurant (or business, for that matter) are:

1.   Idea generation:
   a.   Conviction (willingness): are you willing and able to be an entrepreneur?
   b.   Business idea (focus): do you really believe in your idea? Do you have the ability to execute your idea?

2.   Preparation:
   a.   Business plan (concept/structure): how will the idea be put into practice? (market research, business model, team, advisors, investors, strategy, operation)
   b.   Venture (investment): legal structure, partnerships, incorporation, roles and responsibilities, investment, find IBY (I believe in You) investors, employees, customers)

3.   Execution:
   a.   Business (revenue): make, buy, or ally, institutionalization of systems, evaluate procedures, teams, operations, and financing
   b.   Sustainable business (time): ability to adapt to changing environment/circumstances, maintain or increase performance, continuous renewal.

Clearly, denial in any of these stages is detrimental to the performance of the organization. However, because these stages are cumulative, which means that they build upon one another, denial is more detrimental in the earlier stages. This becomes obvious if we make the comparison with the (psychological) development of a human/individual. Traumatic experiences early in an infant's life often have more detrimental consequences than traumatic experiences at a later stage. The same applies to organizations; denial is more detrimental in the early stages. This is also reflected in the reasons for failure. The number one reason is wrong expectations, which has to do with the conviction and idea stage. The next most important reason for failure is management, which starts in the preparation phase. It goes beyond the scope of this book to go into details for each of these stages, the main point that we need to take into account is that a distorted perception is most lethal in the early phases of the process, as the phases build on one another in a cumulative fashion.

Morphological changes (i.e., the structural alterations to the organization)
These refer to the structural alterations of the organization's elements, or the abnormal condition (i.e., functioning) of the organization. Before these can be delineated, we first need to understand what the normal structure (condition or functioning) is of the organization, just like we need to understand the normal structure (condition or functioning) of a human being before we can identify the alterations due to the disease. In medicine, this refers to the anatomy of the human body, and in a similar vein, we thus need to develop the anatomy of an organization. Therefore, in the next chapter, we will develop an image of a healthy organization, by delineating some of its core principles and characteristics. Once we have established the anatomy of a healthy organization, we can compare it to a failing organization to identify the structural

alterations (i.e., by identifying what is different). As previously mentioned, most important to the equation is the owner of the organization or business, and an analysis of structural alterations should therefore always take a top down approach.

Clinical manifestations (i.e., the symptoms of organizational failure)

These are extremely easy to spot. One visit to the restaurant as a critical consumer or alert observant will immediately reveal the main symptoms, like poor food quality, inconsistency, chaos, unsatisfied customers, complaints, poor communication, empty seats, and stress. More hidden are the symptoms of empty cash registers, sale of owner's personal assets, increasing levels of debt, and impending financial disaster.

The fate of the organization is tied to the fate of the individuals at key positions within the organization (e.g., owner and management), symptoms can also be detected at the individual level. Examples of individual symptoms are, for example, stress, anger, frustration, temper tantrums, irritation, shouting, aggressiveness, and defensiveness. The general principle is that an overreaction towards trivial issues is an indication of high levels of stress. Obviously, this stress can also have other causes, and could be completely independent from the restaurant. However, if symptoms can be identified at the individual and organizational levels at the same time, most likely these are interconnected. Now that we have a somewhat better understanding of the pathology of a failing restaurant, we can continue with the question how to cure this disease. That is, how can we correct the error in the functioning of the organization?

The treatment of disease (i.e., correcting organizational failure)

The treatment of a disease can be modelled using our dynamic feedback control model of Figure 7. This model suggest that an iterative problem solving strategy based on feedback loops is needed to treat the disease. After the treatment, another diagnosis of the patient and/or disease is needed to make sure that the disease is cured and the patient is healed. If so, the exit stage refers to the dismissal of the patient from the hospital and exit from the treatment process. The application of this model of strategy to the treatment of organizational failure is relatively straightforward. In the test or diagnosis stage, there is a comparison between the organization's desired state (or configuration; e.g., Ω^*) and the organization's actual state (e.g., Ω). If this is the case (i.e., $\Omega^* = \Omega^*$), then this part of the organization conforms to our desired state of the organization, and we continue to the next part of the organization. If this is not the case (i.e., $\Omega^* \neq \Omega$), then this part of the organization is changed until the organizational part matches our expectations or desired state. Hence, we operate on (i.e., change) the organizational part, and when it matches our desired state, we exit. Over time, the organization changes or evolves naturally, just like we do as we get older. This means that we need to test occasionally to make sure that the organizational part matches the desired state we have defined for this part (e.g., check up every 2-4 years; this also ties to staff evaluations).

Implications for Big Corporations

While this book is based on turnarounds in small restaurants, there are also invaluable lessons for the management of large enterprises from any business. Most importantly, we think that an organizational turnaround of a large enterprise in reality is not much different or harder than turning around a small restaurant. Gordon Ramsay explains in the episode on D-place that, "If the head chef and the general manager get on then everyone underneath will follow suit." Although the group of people may be somewhat larger, this rule is also applicable to big corporations. If general management gets along, the rest of the organization will follow suit. Changing the direction of even an large enterprise is not that difficult. As long as you start at the top and are willing to put in the effort it can be done. If the CEO is really willing and committed to change, and has the passion, power, and conviction to convince and align the rest of the board, it can be achieved. This is proven by numerous examples of successful turnarounds (e.g., Apple, Chrysler, and Caterpillar) and transformations (e.g., IBM) of multinational enterprises.

Undeniably there are more differences between the turnaround of a large corporation and a small restaurant. The added complexity is mainly caused by three factors. First because large companies are more complicated; they can span multiple cultures, structures and a large set of different power groups. Second, the size of a large company in combination with its complexity often leads to communication difficulties between the top and the lower ranks of the organization in which information is accidentally lost or deliberately left out and misinformation is added by different stakeholders. Third, substantial teams are needed to execute initiatives in a large corporation. Ideas cannot be implemented by a single man. This for instance implies that it may take a while to implement new policies and when they are finally implemented, they are never quite as the top management team intended them to be. Already the diagnosis phase is much more complex. Where a diagnosis within a small business can be done by a single person observing professionals at work, a diagnose in a large corporation requires large teams of specialists adding their own expertise to get a focused overview of the business problem(s).

It should also be noted that in some ways it is even easier to change a large enterprise rather than a small firm. For one thing, due to the separation of ownership (i.e., shareholders) and management (i.e., the CEO and board of directors), management is often much easier to replace than in the case of a small business where ownership and management are often intertwined. If deemed necessary, the management of a large enterprise can be replaced, something that cannot be done with most small- and medium-sized companies. In large enterprises, when the CEO or other directors are non-performing they can be relieved from their function and replaced by more competent others. As such, managers and directors in big corporations are mere temporary agents that can be substituted if need be. There are unquestionably exceptions to this rule, such as family businesses (e.g., IKEA, Samsung, Ford, and Heineken) where the links between owners and daily management are rather strong. An additional advantage that replacing non-performing managers and directors brings is that it becomes much more difficult for the organization to regress into old dysfunctional behavioural patterns.

Overseeing all these arguments we still feel that the key to changing a big corporation can very well be compared with changing a restaurant. This is to start from the top and get the TMT in line. When the turnaround manager is able to align the team, the basic process of confronting failure, provoking and breaking through denial, connecting, creating a shared vision, and implementing necessary changes, is quite similar. Many of the lessons described in this book are generally applicable and are not limited to small and medium business. Even very large multinational corporations can learn a lot from the techniques applied by Gordon Ramsay. The change techniques in this book are relevant for large corporations, but they are hardly used in practice. Have you ever heard of a large organization that puts its departments and divisions under extra stress, just to see where it hurts and to create a case for change? Have you ever seen a large organization that sends overpaid senior managers on an extra vacation just to see what happens with the performance of their department and whether young talents will grab their chance? How many directors are really interested in their key managers and even go to their homes and partners to find out what really makes them tick? How many organizations really listen to the customer and bring the customer closer to the company? Which organizations really focus on the negatives instead? How many organizations are really communicating with the employees in a turnaround instead of sending newsletters around? These are a few examples of elements that we feel are hardly used in corporate transformations and turnarounds. Applying these techniques will improve the lives of millions of owners, managers and employees working in the ever-changing corporate world.

LITERATURE LIST

- Åström, K.J. and R. M. Murray, Feedback systems : an introduction for scientists and engineers, Princeton University Press, Princeton, 2008.
- Babiak, P., Neumann, C. S. and Hare, R. D. (2010), Corporate psychopathy: Talking the walk. *Behav. Sci. Law*, 28: 174–193. doi: 10.1002/bsl.925
- Beckhard, R., 1969, Organization Development: Strategies and Models, Reading, MA: Addison-Wesley.
- Bénabou, R. (2009), Groupthink: Collective Delusions in Organizations and Markets, NBER Working Paper No. 14764.
- Blackledge, T. (2012) Interview with Dr. Tod Blackledge, available online at http://www.uakron.edu/innovation/spiders.dot
- Boxenbaum, E. and Rouleau, L. (2011), New Knowledge Products as Bricolage: Metaphors and Scripts in Organizational Theory, Academy of Management Review, 36(2), pp. 272-296.

- Brandon, N. (2001) The Psychology of Self-Esteem: A revolutionary approach to self-understanding that launched a new era in modern psychology, Jossey-Bass, San Francisco.
- Brosnan, S.F.; de Waal, F.B.M. (2003). "Monkeys reject unequal pay." *Nature* **425** (6955): 297.
- Bynum, W.F. and Porter, R. (eds) (2005) Oxford Dictionary of Scientific Quotations. Oxford University Press. 21:9.
- Carroll, G.R., & Hannan, M.T. (2000) The Demography of Corporations and Industries. Princeton: Princeton University Press.
- Csíkszentmihályi, M. (1990), Flow: The Psychology of Optimal Experience, New York: Harper and Row.
- Cohen, S. (2011). States of Denial: knowing about atrocities and suffering, Wiley.
- Crowley, L. V. (2013). An introduction to human disease: Pathology and pathophysiology correlations. Jones & Bartlett Publishers.
- Daft, R.L., and Lewin, A.Y. (1990), Can organization science begin to break out of the normal science straightjacket? An editorial essay, Organization Science, 1 (1), pp. 1-9.
- Doyle, A.C. (1986). The Complete Sherlock Holmes: All 4 Novels and 56 Short Stories, Bantam Classics.
- Embley, Ken (2005) The Burning Platform, Policy Perspectives, 1(1), available online at: http://www.imakenews.com.
- Ericsson, A.K. (2006), The Scientific Study of Expert Levels of Performance: general implications for optimal learning and creativity, High Ability Studies, 9, 75-100.
- Field, A. (2010) Taking on a Business Partner? Avoid these 4 Common Mistakes, Business Insider, available online at Businessinsider.com.
- Ford, J. D., & Ford, L. W. (2009), Decoding resistance to change, Harvard Business Review, 87, 99-103.

- Glaser, B.G., and Strauss, A.L. (1967) The Discovery of Grounded Theory: Strategies for Qualitative Research, Aldine Transactions, New Jersey, USA.
- Helms M.M. ed., Encyclopedia of Management, Gale Cengage, 2006
- Hyatt, Michael (2012) Four Characteristics of Inspirational Leaders, available online at http://michaelhyatt.com.
- Jainworld (2012) Elephant and the Blind Men, available online at http://www.jainworld.com.
- Janis, Irving L. (1972). Victims of Groupthink. New York: Houghton Mifflin.
- Janis, Irving L. (1982). Groupthink: Psychological Studies of Policy Decisions and Fiascoes. Second Edition. New York: Houghton Mifflin.
- Kadavy, T. (2011) The Power of Observation, available online at http://www.innovationexcellence.com.
- Kanter, R. M., Stein, B. A. and Jick, T. D. (1992), The Challenge of Organizational Change, The Free Press, New York.
- Kaptchuk TJ, Kelley JM, Conboy LA, Davis RB, Kerr CE, Jacobson EE, Kirsch I, Schyner RN, Nam BH, Nguyen LT, Park M, Rivers AL, McManus C, Kokkotou E, Drossman DA, Goldman P, Lembo AJ (2008). Components of placebo effect: randomised controlled trial in patients with irritable bowel syndrome. BMJ 336 (7651): 999–1003.
- Kelly, D. (2001) Product Development Process: Observation, Entrepreneurial Thought Leadership Series, available online at http://ecorner.stanford.edu.
- Knaup, A. (2005). Survival and longevity in the business employment dynamics data. *Monthly Labor Review*, May, 50–56.
- Kotter, J. P. (1996), Leading Change, Harvard Business School Press, Boston, MA.
- Kuhn, T.S. (1962), The Structure of Scientific Revolutions. Chicago: University of Chicago Press.

- Levinson, J.C. (1998), Guerrilla Marketing: Secrets for Making Big Profits from Your Small Business, Houghton Mifflin Company.
- Lewin, K (1947), Frontiers in Group Dynamics, Channels of Group Life; Social Planning and Action Research, Human Relations, 1947, 1, pp. 143-153.
- Merriam Webster (2012), Online Dictionary, Accessed March 2012.
- Niemi, M.B. (2009) Placebo Effect: A Cure in the Mind, Scientific American, February issue.
- Parsa, H.G., Self, J.T., Njite, D., and King, T. (2005) Why Restaurants Fail, Cornell Hotel and Restaurant Administrative Quarterly, August, pp. 304-322.
- Pink, D. H. (2011) Drive: The Surprising Truth about what motivates us, Canongate Books, Edinburgh, UK.
- Popper, K. (2002) The Logic of Scientific Discovery, Routledge, London.
- Ramsay, G. (2008) Humble Pie, HarperCollins Publishers, London.
- Rucci, A. J., Kirn, S. P. and R.T. Quinn (1998). The employee-customer-profit chain at Sears. Harvard Business Review, Jan-Feb, 82-97.
- Schaeffer, P. (2011) The Seven Pitfalls of Business Failure and How to Avoid Them, Businessknowhow.com, January.
- Schumpeter, J.A. (1934) The Theory of Economic Development: An inquiry into profits, capital, credit, interest and the business cycle, Transaction Publishers, New Jersey, USA.
- Shein, J.B. (2011) Reversing the Slide: A strategic guide to turnarounds and corporate renewal, Jossey Bass, San Francisco.
- Shontell, A. (2011) 10 Super Successful Cofounders and Why Their Partnership Worked, Business Insider, available online at Businessinsider.com.
- Smith, Adam (1977) An Inquiry into the Nature and Causes of the Wealth of Nations. University Of Chicago Press, Chicago.
- Sun Tzu (1971), The Art of War, Oxford University Press

- Tedlow, R. (2010) Denial: Why Business Leaders Fail to Look Facts in the Face—and What to Do About It, Portfolio.
- Thomas, G. and James, D. (2006). Reinventing grounded theory: some questions about theory, ground and discovery, British Educational Research Journal, 32 (6), pp. 767–795.
- Van Witteloostuijn, A. (1995) Laat duizend bloemen bloeien, Inaugural Lecture at Maastricht University, Academic Service, Schoonhoven
- Wastyn, A., & Hussinger, K. (2011, February). Search for the not-invented-here syndrome: The role of knowledge sources and firm success. Paper for the 2001 DRUID Conference.
- Welch, J., & Byrne, J.A. (2003) Jack: Straight from the Gut, Warner Books, New York.
- Weitzel, W., and Johnson, E. (1989) Decline in Organizations: A literature integration and extension, Administrative Science Quarterly, 34, pp. 91-109.
- Zimmerman, F.M. (1991), The Turnaround Experience: Real World Lessons in Revitalizing Corporations, McGrawHill.

INDEX OF CITED RESTAURANTS

Anna Vincenzo's, 171
Bazzini, 214, 244
Black Pearl, 74, 143
Bonapartes Restaurant, 217
Campania, 120, 157, 185, 236, 239
Casa Roma, 84
Classic American, 84, 87
Clubway 41, 128, 212, 221, 243
Davide, 200
Dillon's, 61, 75, 83, 165, 244
Down City, 118, 137, 268
D-place, 65, 127, 129, 154, 155, 170, 184, 274
Fiesta Sunrise, 82, 112, 168, 218
Finn McCool's, 89, 180, 199
Fleming, 218
Giuseppi's, 143
Grasshopper Also, 84

Hot Potato Café, 89, 95, 192, 244
J Willy's, 223
La Gondola, 16, 17, 56, 133, 194, 239, 243
La Lanterna, 46, 88, 100, 115, 135, 136, 137, 169, 194, 235, 244
La Parra de Burriana, 50, 84, 127, 137, 142, 193, 195, 235
La Riviera, 85, 111, 120, 128, 133, 146, 183, 194, 200, 213, 218, 236, 269
Le Bistro, 159
Lela's, 34, 171
Lido di Manhattan Beach, 147, 171, 244
Momma Cherri's Soul Food Shack, 45, 56, 88, 215
Moore Place, 54, 114, 213, 214
Morgan's, 66, 70, 75, 89, 138, 158, 169, 226

Oscar's, 60, 89, 127, 133, 186, 194, 200
Peter's, 46, 89, 170, 203, 205
Piccolo Teatro, 34, 88, 131, 133, 212, 222, 227, 233
PJ's Steakhouse, 84, 119, 133, 144
Rococo, 85, 138, 170, 171, 172, 174, 201, 209
Ruby Tate, 85, 98, 155, 171
Sabiatello's, 117, 194
Santé La Brea, 84
Seascape, 34, 89, 113, 175
Sebastian's, 34, 170
Spanish Pavilion, 83, 124, 218
Sushi-Ko, 124, 129, 194
The Curry Lounge, 57, 78, 193, 195, 222
The Dovecote Bistro, 42, 89, 114, 158, 174, 209

The Fenwick Arms, 62, 208, 226, 232
The Fish and Anchor, 80, 139, 197
The Glass House, 61, 178, 180, 224
The Granary, 48, 63, 73, 126, 170, 194
The Mixing Bowl, 66, 92, 170
The Olde Stone Mill, 114, 170
The Priory, 84, 98, 128, 170, 193, 194, 241
The Runaway Girl, 70, 71, 113, 170, 171, 233, 242
The Sandgate Hotel, 46, 75, 85, 88, 89, 134, 212, 214, 236, 242, 243
The Secret Garden, 51, 122, 141, 144, 238, 239
The Walnut Tree Inn, 34, 179, 227
Trobiano's, 133, 239

www.ingramcontent.com/pod-product-compliance
Lightning Source LLC
Chambersburg PA
CBHW061142220326
41599CB00025B/4324